CLAIRE MACDONALD'S
QUICK & EASY
DESSERTS
AND PUDDINGS

Published by BBC Books, a division of
BBC Enterprises Limited, Woodlands,
80 Wood Lane, London W12 0TT

First published 1993
Copyright © Claire Macdonald 1993

ISBN 0 563 36443 2

Designed by Peter Bridgewater
Photographs by James Murphy
Styling by Jane McLish
Home Economist Allyson Birch

Typeset by BP Integraphics Ltd, Bath, Avon
Printed and bound in Great Britain by Clays Ltd, St Ives plc
Colour separations by Technik Ltd, Berkhamsted
Cover printed by Clays Ltd, St Ives plc

Claire Macdonald, High Chief of Clan Donald, is a well-known cookery writer. In 1982 she won the Glenfiddich Cookery Writer of the Year award.

Quick and Easy Puddings and Desserts is Claire's tenth book. Previous titles include the *Harrods Book of Entertaining* and *Lady Macdonald's Chocolate Book*. She also writes for newspapers and journals including the *Glasgow Weekend Times*, the *Aberdeen Press and Journal* and *The Field*.

Claire Macdonald is married to Lord Macdonald and with him runs the Kinloch Lodge Country House Hotel on the Isle of Skye. She has four children.

CLAIRE MACDONALD'S
QUICK & EASY
DESSERTS
AND PUDDINGS

BBC BOOKS

BBC BOOKS' QUICK AND EASY COOKERY SERIES

Launched in 1989 by Ken Hom and Sarah Brown, the *Quick and Easy Cookery* series is a culinary winner. Everything about the titles is aimed at quick and easy recipes – the ingredients, the cooking methods and the menu section at the back of the books. Eight pages of colour photographs are also included to provide a flash of inspiration for the frantic or faint-hearted.

OTHER TITLES IN THE SERIES ALREADY PUBLISHED:

Beverley Piper's Quick and Easy Healthy Cookery ★ *Clare Connery's Quick and Easy Salads* ★ *Joanna Farrow's Quick and Easy Fish Cookery* ★ *Ken Hom's Quick and Easy Chinese Cookery* ★ *Sandeep Chatterjee's Quick and Easy Indian Vegetarian Cookery* ★ *Sarah Brown's Quick and Easy Vegetarian Cookery* ★ *Shaun Hill's Quick and Easy Vegetable Cookery* ★

TO COME:

Joanna Farrow's Quick and Easy Cake Decorating ★ *Madhur Jaffrey's Quick and Easy Indian Cookery* ★ *Mary Berry's Quick and Easy Cakes* ★ *Linda Fraser's Quick and Easy Suppers* ★

CONTENTS

INTRODUCTION 9

STOCKING UP 11

THE STORE-CUPBOARD 12

KITCHEN EQUIPMENT 15

QUICK COLD PUDDINGS 17

QUICK HOT PUDDINGS 39

FROZEN PUDDINGS 61

QUICK PUDDINGS FOR ENTERTAINING 83

SAUCES 119

INDEX 127

INTRODUCTION

For me, there are three types of quick pudding (sweet, or dessert, call it what you will). First of all there is the pudding you make at the drop of a hat using store-cupboard ingredients. These are usually made for unexpected guests, but also on occasions they are useful when you feel like a sweet course out of the blue. A delicious example of this type of impromptu pud is Lychees in Crème de Menthe (see p. 112).

The second kind is a pudding which is quick and simple to assemble at the last minute, but which has had a little more time spent on its concoction at a previous time when it was convenient for you. All the frozen puddings come into this category and so do the meringues. None of them takes very long to put together and they are so handy to have already prepared. There is this fallacy that busy people just like to reach for a packet of something and cover it with whipped cream flavoured with, perhaps, lemon or alcohol and call it a pudding. However, it is my experience that a great many busy people love to cook and see it as a form of relaxation and creativity. What they need to be able to do is to plan when to make the dishes to fit into their busy schedule. So I hope that there will be plenty of recipes within this book which will help and inspire such cooks to create delicious desserts at their own convenience.

The third category of recipes are those which can actually be made quickly, usually taking 10 minutes at the most in the actual preparation, but which need to be cooked or left to cool or set in a fridge for a few hours. The puddings which require cooking can either be made the day before they are needed and then gently reheated (for example, the rice puddings, fruity crumbles, and the Hot Dried Fruit Salad, see p. 60) or the dish can be prepared with the rest of your meal and cooked in the time it takes to dish up and eat the main course (for example Baked Spiced Pineapple Cake, see p. 53, or Baked Mincemeat-stuffed Pears, see p. 57). You just need to choose the most convenient time. The dishes which need time in a fridge to set or cool obviously need to be thought of in advance but they are all extremely speedy in the making and then look after themselves until needed at table!

I have also included a small selection of quick sauces, ideal to dress up vanilla ice-cream, which must surely be the quickest pudding in the book.

I thought long and hard about the possible contents of the store-cupboard but as I say in the introduction to the chapter on the store-cupboard, I *don't* mean that you should stock each one of the items listed! But if you have some of them in stock you will never be stuck for a quick pudding.

Quantities are always difficult because appetites vary so much for a variety of reasons – a lot depends on the preceding course. Generally speaking, most people won't feel like eating very much pudding following, for example, steak and kidney pie. Elderly guests or elderly members of your family probably won't eat as much as half the amount that a teenager will eat (and if you are cooking for teenage *boys*, I advise you to double the quantity of anything you make!).

There are certain pieces of equipment which make life in the kitchen that little bit easier. Top of the list are sharp knives – a straight-bladed one and a serrated one (the latter for slicing peel off citrus fruit). But other time-savers include a good potato peeler (ideal for shaving chocolate off a block for decoration) and a good grater. So often people forget that graters blunt and if yours is stainless steel and you have had it for some time, it will most probably be blunt. My advice is to throw your old one away and buy another. The cost involved is minimal when you consider how much easier your life will be. A food processor is invaluable. Even if you don't cook very often, I guarantee that once you own a food processor you will discover more and more things that you can make, grate and slice in it. A good piping bag with one large star-shaped nozzle and one plain nozzle may sound like an unnecessary extra to those of you who are not very experienced in the kitchen but, believe me, they really are worth having. It is so much quicker to pipe things like meringues onto a baking tray, rather than trying to spoon them on. Piping whipped cream as a decoration also becomes a matter of seconds. One tip about washing the piping bag – turn it inside out and sluice it down under running hot water, then put it into your washing machine on a hot wash.

The recipes in this book have been written to help anyone who leads a busy life to make wonderful desserts. Each day that passes seems to have fewer hours than the last and as desserts are a luxury they often seem to get lost! I'm sure that the recipes I have put together here will whet your appetite and inspire you to make them. But most important of all I hope you find the time to really *enjoy* them.

STOCKING UP

If your store-cupboard contained all the items I list below it would be a veritable Aladdin's cave, full of inspiration for the would-be pudding cook with little time to concoct a sweet dish. It would also need to be quite large. But with just a few of the things in stock, in cupboard, freezer and drinks' cupboard, it should be a matter of seconds to select from this book and make a quick pud.

One thing to beware of in a store-cupboard: certain items like brandy snaps, sponge fingers or trifle sponges do have a sell-by date on them, so don't buy several packets and keep them for months. From time to time check on their sell-by dates and make sure that you use them up. That in itself can be a deciding factor on the recipe you choose!

Ground spices are the other thing which do not benefit from an endless spell of time in a cupboard. Many people just don't realize how much ready ground spices deteriorate, to the extent that after a few months you need more and more spice to get more than a hint of flavour from it. Whole nutmegs, on the other hand, keep for years in a screw-topped jar, and they take a second to grind on a grater. For the most part, whole spices have a very much longer shelf-life than those which are ready ground. Nuts, too, go stale over a period of time. You can, however, refresh them to a certain extent by dry-frying them for several minutes, before including them in a recipe.

Alcohol keeps indefinitely – until it is drunk! And the five bottles I list can all be adapted to embellish many of the recipes within this book. If you were to choose just one alcohol out of the five, I would opt for brandy, for its wider range of use than the others.

THE STORE-CUPBOARD

Honey
Strawberry jam
Raspberry jam
Cherry jam
Ginger marmalade
Golden syrup
1 or 2 jars of mincemeat
Jar of preserved ginger in syrup
Tins of lychees
Tins of pineapple chunks
Tins of cherries

DRY GOODS

Self-raising flour
Demerara sugar
Caster sugar
Icing sugar
Granulated sugar
Cornflour
Arrowroot
Custard powder
Gelatine
1 or 2 packets of dried dates
Packet of sultanas
Glacé cherries
Desiccated coconut
1 or 2 packets of walnut halves
1 or 2 packets of flaked almonds
1 or 2 packets of ground almonds
1 or 2 packets of pecan nuts
Digestive biscuits

Gingernuts
1 or 2 packets of brandy snaps
Sponge fingers
Trifle sponges
Ready-made pancakes or crêpes
Meringue nests
Porridge oats or pinhead oatmeal (if available)

FLAVOURINGS

Bottle of lemon juice
Bottle of rennet
Vanilla essence
Ground ginger
Ground cinnamon
Whole nutmegs
Whole cardamoms
1 or 2 bars good dark chocolate

FRIDGE

Butter
Cream
Milk
Eggs
Greek yoghurt
Carton of fresh custard

FREEZER

Shortcrust pastry
Malt loaves
Good vanilla ice-cream

DRINKS

Brandy
Sherry
Rum
Crème de Menthe
Cointreau

KITCHEN EQUIPMENT

I think that probably the most vital piece of kitchen equipment for any type of cooking preparation, savoury or sweet, is a really sharp knife. For preparing fruit, a small-bladed knife is essential. An apple corer and a cherry stoner are also useful, although not essential (you can core apples, even for stuffing, with a small sharp knife). Use a serrated-edged knife for cutting meringues and cakes of all types. Hard plastic spatulas for easy scraping out of bowls and a good palette knife are also helpful.

A food processor is good for pulverizing biscuits into crumbs to make pie bases, as well as for grating chocolate and you can mix cake batters using the plastic blade. But you'll also find a small hand-held or electric whisk of use when beating small quantities of egg-white or cake mixture.

For some recipes you'll need a large piping bag. It's useful to have two nozzles one a plain small-ended nozzle, the other a squashed star-shaped nozzle. These are useful for piping meringues, as well as filling brandy snaps, and the piping bag can be easily washed by being put on a hot wash in your machine.

A selection of large and small metal or pyrex mixing bowls is essential when making puddings and desserts. I prefer to steer clear of plastic mixing bowls (apart from my huge plastic bread-making bowl). You'll also find that two or three pretty serving bowls in china or glass and a selection of ramekins and pretty individual serving dishes or glasses give lots of opportunity to make any dessert look attractive.

QUICK COLD PUDDINGS

I wish that the days of a final sweet course weren't over – decades ago lunch, supper or dinner wouldn't have been considered complete without a pudding of some sort to finish the meal. I know I am not alone in loving to end any meal on a sweet note, and the recipes in this chapter are for people like me. They are all very quick to make. Once made, some of them do need to sit for several hours but they look after themselves – like the junkets. Most of them involve fruit, like the Strawberry and Banana Fool (see p. 23), and the Blackberry, Apple and Lemon Jelly (see p. 27). If a meal has more than one course to it, quite apart from the delicious eating there is the added benefit of prolonging the length of time spent by the family or friends sitting round the table together. For me, mealtimes are the best times of the day and, whenever practical, never to be hurried but to be as drawn out as possible. By serving a pudding this is one way to do just that!

CONTENTS

JUNKET *19*

CHOCOLATE AND COFFEE JUNKET *20*

CARAMEL ORANGES *21*

PEARS WITH MULLED WINE SAUCE *22*

STRAWBERRY AND BANANA FOOL

MERINGUES *24*

AUTUMN PUDDING *25*

GOOSEBERRY AND ELDERFLOWER FOOL *26*

BLACKBERRY, APPLE AND LEMON JELLY *27*

FRESH PINAPPLE AND GINGER CREAM *28*

CHOCOLATE MARSHMALL PIE *29*

CRANBERRY AND ORANGE WHIP *30*

BLACK CHERRY CREAMY DELIGHT *31*

MOCHA BROWNIES *32*

FRUIT SALAD WITH HONEY AND LEMON DRESSING *35*

RASPBERRY WHIP *36*

SPICED APPLE AND HONEY MOUSSE *37*

CREAM, YOGHURT AND GRAPE PUDDING *38*

JUNKET

SERVES

—— 2 ——

Junket is a very old-fashioned pudding, but one of the simplest and most delicious, especially when eaten with thick cream as an embellishment. It is the sort of pudding that can be made in about 2 minutes, although it needs several hours to set before being eaten. You can make it at breakfast time and then leave it all ready for supper that evening, by which time the milk will have thickened. This amount is for two people, and I like to dish it in two glasses. Two tips about making junket: don't put the dish (or glasses) of junket into the fridge until the milk is cooled; and if the amount of rennet seems excessive to the quantity of milk, it is because milk is virtually all pasteurized these days (unless you have your own cow) and therefore more rennet is necessary than used to be needed with unpasteurized milk. Rennet is easily obtainable from chemists.

Warm the milk to blood heat – that is, when you stick your finger into the milk and it feels neither hot nor cool. Take the pan off the heat, stir in the rennet and sugar, pour into the glasses and grate a little nutmeg over the surface of each. When cooled put in the fridge for a few hours until the milk has thickened.

INGREDIENTS

300 ml (10 fl oz) milk
2 teaspoons rennet
2 teaspoons caster sugar
A little freshly grated
  nutmeg

CHOCOLATE AND COFFEE JUNKET

SERVES

—— 2 ——

INGREDIENTS

300 ml (10 fl oz) milk
2 teaspoons dark chocolate,
grated
½ teaspoon instant coffee
granules
1 teaspoon caster sugar
2 teaspoons rennet

This is a variation on the plain Junket (see p. 19), and adds only about half a minute onto the preparation and cooking time.

Put the milk into a pan together with the grated chocolate and the instant coffee. Warm gently till the milk reaches blood heat and the chocolate begins to melt in the warmth and the coffee to dissolve. Stir it to hurry this along. Take the pan off the heat and stir in the sugar and rennet. Pour into two glasses and when cool leave in the fridge for several hours to set.

CARAMEL ORANGES

SERVES

— 6 —

9 oranges, peeled
225 g (8 oz) granulated
sugar

Probably because I love citrus fruit, this is one of my favourite puddings. How you slice the oranges depends on how much time you have, but it really doesn't take much longer to slice them into segments, cutting between the skin which divides each segment from one another, than it does to slice them across. If you do slice them across, you need only 6 oranges for the same number of people.

Carefully slice the skin off the oranges, using a serrated knife. Slice over a serving dish to catch the juice which drips from the oranges as you cut – this juice is used to soften the caramel as the oranges sit waiting to be eaten. Place the prepared oranges in the serving dish.

Meanwhile, put the sugar into a heavy-based, large pan (the wider the surface of the pan the quicker the sugar will melt). Over a moderate heat dissolve the sugar, shaking the pan from time to time, but don't be tempted to stir the sugar as it melts. Also don't be tempted to hurry the procedure by turning up the heat, because burnt sugar has a bitter taste which can't be disguised. Providing you use a wide-based pan it won't take a minute to caramelize. Shake the pan till you have an even golden-brown caramel, then pour this over the prepared oranges in the serving dish.

PEARS WITH MULLED WINE SAUCE

SERVES

— 6 —

FOR THE SAUCE:
450 ml (15 fl oz) red wine
150 ml (5 fl oz) water
Pared rind of 1 orange
1 cinnamon stick
3–4 cloves
75 g (3 oz) granulated sugar
2 rounded teaspoons arrowroot
3 tablespoons cold water

6 large, ripe pears – use 8 if the pears are small

I like fruity based puddings at the end of a lunch or dinner menu because that allows more leeway with richness in the preceding two courses. This pudding, ideal in the autumn when British pears are in season, makes a delicious finale to a rich and filling meal. If the pears are juicy and ripe there is no need to cook them, but beware their tendency to discolour when they are peeled and cored – this can be avoided by brushing them with lemon juice. Make the mulled wine sauce first, so that it is all ready to pour over the sliced pears.

Put the wine, water, orange rind (I use a potato peeler to pare it, to avoid any of the bitter white pith), cinnamon stick, cloves and sugar into a pan and heat gently, stirring, till the sugar dissolves. Leave for 5 minutes on the heat. Meanwhile, peel and core and slice the pears and place in a serving dish. Then shake the arrowroot into the cold water, add a little of the hot liquid from the pan to it, stir well, then pour this into the pan and stir over heat till the sauce boils. As it bubbles and thickens the cloudy appearance gives way to a clear, jewel-coloured sauce. Pour through a sieve over the sliced pears in the dish. Serve warm or cold.

STRAWBERRY AND BANANA FOOL

SERVES

— 6 —

It was only a few years ago that I realized what a good combination are strawberries and bananas. It can be particularly useful if you only have a limited quantity of strawberries and need to pad out the amount for un-expected guests. It's also useful if the strawberries are slightly mushy. And most important of all, it's delicious!

Peel the bananas and break them into a liquidizer or food processor. Add the hulled strawberries and whiz till you have a fairly smooth purée. Fold this into the whipped cream, taste, and add a little sieved icing sugar if you think the mixture needs it. If the strawberries are ripe and sweet it shouldn't be necessary to add any sugar. Either pour and scrape the fool into a glass or china serving bowl, or divide between individual serving glasses. Keep, covered, in the fridge till you are ready to serve it or eat it immediately!

INGREDIENTS

4 bananas
450 g (1 lb) strawberries, hulled
300 ml (10 fl oz) double cream, whipped
Icing sugar to taste (optional)

MERINGUES

SERVES

—— 6–8 ——

4 egg whites
225 g (8 oz) caster sugar

I am including meringues in this book because although they take a couple of hours to cook, they take about 3 minutes to make. They freeze extremely well, and can also be kept for up to two weeks in an air-tight container. They are loved by every single person I know and need only to be sandwiched together with whipped cream to make an instant, last-minute pudding. If you have the time and inclination you can embellish the cream with a liqueur or grated dark chocolate as you whip it.

Pre-heat the oven to gas mark ¼, 225°F (110°C).

Put the whites into a clean bowl and whisk them – I find a hand-held electric whisk the most useful way to do this. When the whites are very stiff add the sugar a spoonful at a time, still whisking, and whisk till the sugar is all incorporated. Line 2 baking trays with baking parchment, and pipe (using a wide star-shaped nozzle) or spoon the meringue mixture into even-sized rounds on the lined trays. Bake in the oven for 2 hours. When cooked they should lift easily off the baking parchment. Cool, then store in air-tight containers or the freezer till needed.

*A*UTUMN PUDDING

S E R V E S

—— 6–8 ——

This is a variation on a summer pudding. The flavours of the brambles (or blackberries), damsons, and the good eating apples which are in season in the autumn all combine so very well. Although the pudding needs to be made at least a day in advance it only takes minutes to put together. It keeps very well in the fridge for up to 4 days, or you can make it even further ahead and freeze it. (Allow 2 hours at room temperature to thaw.) Serve it with whipped cream or Greek yoghurt.

INGREDIENTS

6–8 slices of white bread, without crusts
225 g (8 oz) damsons
450 g (1 lb) brambles
450 g (1 lb) Cox's or similar good eating apples, peeled, cored and chopped
225 g (8 oz) soft brown sugar

Line the base and sides of a 1.2-litre (2-pint) pudding bowl with some of the sliced bread. Put the damsons into a saucepan with 300 ml (10 fl oz) water, cover and simmer gently for about 5 minutes. Then fish out the stones using a slotted spoon and a fork. Add the brambles, chopped apples and sugar to the pan and cook gently, covered, for a further 5 minutes. Then take the fruit off the heat. Spoon half the fruit into the bread-lined bowl. Cover with a layer of sliced bread. Put the remaining fruit into the bowl and cover with the rest of the sliced bread. Put a saucer on top and a weight – I use a large tin of tomatoes or similar. Put the bowl into the fridge at least overnight. To serve, turn the pudding out into a serving bowl.

GOOSEBERRY AND ELDERFLOWER FOOL

S E R V E S

—— 6–8 ——

INGREDIENTS

750 g (1½ lb) gooseberries
300 ml (10 fl oz) water
100 g (4 oz) granulated
* sugar*
2 tablespoons elderflower
* cordial*
300 ml (10 fl oz) double
* cream, lightly whipped*
Icing sugar to taste
* (optional)*

Thanks to the availability of delicious elderflower cordial we now no longer need to wait until the elder is in season to use elderflower in our cooking. It is also much quicker and easier too. Elderflower is such a really exquisite taste and one which enhances the flavour of gooseberries. You can use frozen or fresh gooseberries in the recipe.

Put the gooseberries into a saucepan with the water and gently simmer, covered, till the gooseberries are soft. Then add the sugar and elderflower cordial and simmer for a couple of minutes, till the sugar has dissolved completely. Take the pan off the heat and cool. Then liquidize and sieve the purée. Fold together the purée and whipped cream, taste, and add a little icing sugar if you think it isn't sweet enough. Spoon and scrape into serving glasses or a serving bowl. Keep in fridge until needed.

BLACKBERRY, APPLE AND LEMON JELLY

SERVES
—— 6–8 ——

Lemon is a flavour which enhances the taste of fruit such as blackberries (or brambles), strawberries, blackcurrants and raspberries, without becoming a predominant taste itself. This jelly is not a clear jelly, more a set fruit purée, and it can be made either in individual glasses, or in one serving bowl. It can even be made in a loaf or terrine tin and turned out and sliced to serve. (If you decide to do this you need to use 1½ sachets of gelatine.) It is very good with whipped cream, slightly sweetened, or with Greek yoghurt or fromage frais. Crisp biscuits or meringues eaten with it provide a delicious contrasting crunch.

————————

Put the blackberries and pieces of apple into a saucepan with 600 ml (1 pint) water and gently simmer till the blackberries are soft and the pieces of apple can be squished against the sides of the pan with your wooden spoon. Take the pan off the heat, stir in the gelatine and water (which will have sponged up) and the sugar, lemon rind and juice, and liquidize. Sieve the resulting purée, and pour to set into whichever container you have chosen. The jelly can be kept, covered, in the fridge for 2–3 days.

INGREDIENTS

750 g (1½ lb) blackberries
3 dessert apples, such as Cox's, roughly chopped
1 sachet gelatine sprinkled over 3 tablespoons cold water
100 g (4 oz) granulated sugar
Grated rind and juice of 1 lemon

FRESH PINEAPPLE AND GINGER CREAM

SERVES

—— 6–8 ——

INGREDIENTS

1 medium to large-sized
 pineapple
300 ml (10 fl oz) double
 cream
300 ml (10 fl oz) natural
 or Greek yoghurt
About 6 pieces of preserved
 ginger, drained of its
 syrup
2 tablespoons of the ginger
 syrup
75 g (3 oz) good dark
 chocolate, grated

The tang of the fresh pineapple goes so well with the taste of the ginger and with the grated dark chocolate which covers this pudding. The grated chocolate is not just for decoration, it really is an integral part of the dish. The easiest way to grate it is using the grating attachment of a food processor. Otherwise put the chocolate in the fridge for an hour or so and hold it in foil as you hand-grate it – the foil is a bad conductor of heat and so prevents the warmth of your hand from melting the chocolate. Another way to get curls of chocolate is to pare off the chocolate using a potato peeler.

Slice the skin off the pineapple, nicking out the little tuft-like bits of skin from the flesh. Cut the pineapple in half lengthways, then in quarters, and slice away the tough core. Chop the flesh into quite small bits. Whip the cream, but not too stiffly, and fold it and the yoghurt together. Chop the ginger, and fold it with the syrup and the chopped pineapple into the cream and yoghurt. Pour into a glass or china serving bowl. Sprinkle the grated chocolate over the surface, as evenly as you can. Cover the bowl and leave in the fridge till you are ready to serve it.

CHOCOLATE MARSHMALLOW PIE

SERVES
—— 6–8 ——

This is so good for two reasons. The first is that I love just about anything containing chocolate. The second reason is that the pie has a good contrast in texture, between the smooth filling and the crisp crust. And it takes a very short time to make – you can make the filling while the base is baking. This pie can be made a day in advance and kept in the fridge without spoiling in any way. If you want to decorate it, you can grate more dark chocolate over the surface.

Pre-heat the oven to gas mark 4, 350°F (180°C).

Mix together the biscuit crumbs and melted butter and press around the base and sides of a 20-cm (8–in) flan dish. Bake for 10 minutes. Take out and cool.

Put the chocolate, broken into bits, into a heatproof bowl and add the marshmallows and the cream. Put the bowl over a saucepan of gently simmering water till the chocolate and the marshmallows melt. Stir the melted mixture, and pour into the cooled chocolate pie crust. Leave to set.

INGREDIENTS

1 packet dark chocolate digestive biscuits, crushed to crumbs
75 g (3 oz) butter, melted

FOR THE FILLING:
175 g (6 oz) good plain chocolate
1 packet of plain marshmallows
150 ml (5 fl oz) double cream

CRANBERRY AND ORANGE WHIP

SERVES

— 6 —

750 g (1½ lb) cranberries
1 sachet gelatine sprinkled over 3 tablespoons cold water
100 g (4 oz) granulated sugar
2 oranges, peeled and chopped
300 ml (10 fl oz) double cream

Cranberries have a sharp taste which is positively refreshing during the winter months in any form of pudding or finale to a rich cold-weather menu. The taste of cranberries is greatly complemented by orange, and in this quick pudding the cranberries are cooked then liquidized with peeled, chopped oranges. The resulting purée is folded into whipped cream. You can use fresh or frozen cranberries for the recipe.

Put the cranberries into a saucepan and cover. Over a gentle heat cook the cranberries till they are soft, then take them off the heat and stir in the sponged-up gelatine mixture till the gelatine dissolves. Stir in the sugar, let the fruit cool, then liquidize, adding the chopped oranges to the liquidizer with the cranberries. Whip the cream, but not too stiffly, and fold together with the cranberry purée. Pour and scrape into a serving bowl, cover, and leave in a fridge for several hours or overnight before serving.

BLACK CHERRY CREAMY DELIGHT

SERVES
— 6 —

This couldn't be simpler. It's a variation on the whipped cream and yoghurt-type pudding on p. 86. If cherries are in season, and if you have the time and inclination, you can substitute fresh cherries for the tinned ones in the recipe, but they must be stoned.

Whip the cream, but not too stiffly. Fold together the whipped cream, cherry yoghurt, and the cherries. Scrape this mixture into a glass or china serving bowl. Sprinkle the sugar over the surface as evenly as possible. The only way to do this evenly is to use your fingers – this also helps to crush any lumps of sugar. If you try to sieve the sugar it will take an age, so fingers are best! Cover the bowl, and put it into the fridge till needed.

INGREDIENTS

300 ml (10 fl oz) double cream
300 ml (10 fl oz) black cherry yoghurt
1 tin of stoned black cherries, drained
or 225 g (8 oz) fresh cherries
3 tablespoons soft dark brown sugar

MOCHA BROWNIES

SERVES

— 6 —

INGREDIENTS

100 g (4 oz) butter
100 g (4 oz) dark
  chocolate, broken into
  bits
225 g (8 oz) soft brown
  sugar
4 eggs, beaten
175 g (6 oz) plain flour,
  sieved
40 g (1½ oz) cocoa powder
1 tablespoon coffee powder
  or granules

These fudgey textured brownies are different to most brownie recipes in that there is coffee in the mixture as well as chocolate. As most people with a sweet tooth are very well aware, the flavours of chocolate and coffee go extremely well together. I like to serve brownies with vanilla ice-cream as a pudding. This recipe is so easy to make and the brownies keep well in a tin or even freeze successfully – allow 1 hour at room temperature to thaw them.

Pre-heat the oven to gas mark 4, 350°F (180°C).

Put the butter and dark chocolate into a saucepan and melt over a gentle heat. Beat in the sugar and eggs, one by one, and then the sieved flour and cocoa and coffee powder or granules. Grease a 25 × 20 cm (10 in by 8 in) baking tin and line the base of it with baking parchment. Scrape the brownie mixture into it and bake for about 20 minutes until a skewer stuck into the middle of the brownies comes out gooey *not* clean. This ensures the fudgey texture. Cool the brownies in their tin before cutting them into squares and storing them till needed.

LEMON AND COINTREAU WATER ICE-FILLED
ORANGE SHELLS (*page 74*)

FRUIT SALAD WITH HONEY AND LEMON DRESSING

SERVES
— 4 —

Making fruit salad needn't be the laborious job you might suppose. A fruit salad, that is, arranged on individual plates, looks particularly attractive, is low in calories and is an ideal dessert to end a heavy meal. It's quicker than you think to prepare too!

Slice the melon into long, thin slices and cut off the skin. Arrange these slices on the plates.

With a serrated knife slice the skin from the oranges. Slice in towards the centre of each orange, between the pith, to get neat segments. Divide and arrange these on each of the plates.

Hull and halve the strawberries and then arrange them in small heaps.

Carefully slice the skin from the kiwi fruit, slice them into circles, then arrange them on the plates with the rest of the fruit.

Into a small saucepan put the lemon juice and honey. Heat gently until the honey has dissolved then pour this over each plate of arranged fruit.

Garnish, if you like, with sprigs of mint. Applemint is especially good.

INGREDIENTS

½ melon, e.g. honeydew
2 oranges
450 g (1 lb) strawberries
2 kiwi fruit
2 tablespoons honey
juice of 1 lemon
mint or applemint

AUTUMN PUDDING (*page 25*)

RASPBERRY WHIP

SERVES
—— 4–6 ——

450 g (1 lb) raspberries
600 ml (1 pint) fromage
  frais
50 g (2 oz) caster sugar
4 tablespoons demerara
  sugar

The longest part of making this delectable pud is the time it takes you to wash up the food processor! It's at its best when it has been allowed to sit for several hours in the fridge, so it's ideal to make this dessert in the morning ready for an evening meal.

Put the raspberries and fromage frais into a food processor and whiz, adding the caster sugar. When all is well combined – I think it looks good if the raspberries are still in streaky pink bits through the fromage frais – spoon into a serving bowl or into individual glasses.

Sprinkle the demerara sugar evenly over the surface. If possible, leave to rest in the fridge before serving.

SPICED APPLE AND HONEY MOUSSE

S E R V E S
—— 4–6 ——

This is quick to make but benefits from being made several hours or even a day in advance so the flavours have a chance to mingle. It makes the perfect finale to a rich meal as it does not contain either cream or egg yolks. This recipe is an ideal mousse for those on dairy-free diets.

———

Peel and core the apples then chop them. Cook them in a saucepan with the cinnamon, water, lemon juice and honey, until the apples are just beginning to disintegrate. Sprinkle in the gelatine and stir until the granules dissolve. Liquidise and cool.

Whisk the whites until they are stiff. Still whisking, gradually sprinkle in the sugar. Fold into the cooled apples. Serve either in individual dishes or in one large serving bowl.

INGREDIENTS

2 large cooking apples
1 teaspoon ground cinnamon
300 ml (10 fl oz) cold water containing 2 tablespoons lemon juice
2 tablespoons thick or runny honey
2 teaspoons powdered gelatine
2 large egg whites
50 g (2 oz) caster sugar

CREAM, YOGHURT AND GRAPE PUDDING

SERVES

—— 6–8 ——

INGREDIENTS

450 g (1 lb) green or black
  grapes, halved and de-
  pipped
300 ml (10 fl oz) double
  cream, lightly whipped
600 ml (1 pint) natural or
  Greek yoghurt
4–5 tablespoons demerara
  sugar

There are so many variations on this theme but this, I think, is my favourite. You can use soft brown sugar if you prefer (or if you are out of demerara) but I like demerara best of all. It is simplicity itself to make. You need really good, sweet grapes and, for speed, try to get seedless ones.

Put the grape halves into a serving bowl or, if you prefer, you can put them into individual serving bowls or dishes. Mix together the whipped cream and yoghurt and spoon and scrape over the grapes. Sprinkle the demerara sugar as evenly as possible over the surface.

QUICK HOT PUDDINGS

Strong men wilt in anticipation of a hot pudding – and so do a great number of women too. There is something so intensely comforting about hot puddings. Perhaps some of them have nursery connotations, like the Rich and Quick Bread and Butter Pudding (see p. 42), whilst others are just rather wicked, like the Baked Vanilla Sponge with Chocolate Sauce (see p. 52) or the Toasted Coconut Slice with the Cherry Jam Sauce (see pp. 51 and 121). Other recipes are delicious as well as distinctly healthy, like the Hot Dried Fruit Salad (see p. 60) or the Baked Dried Apricots with Orange and Ginger (see p. 45). All of the recipes are easy to make, some can be made in advance and reheated gently before serving. Some, like the Hot Fresh Fruit Salad (see p. 46), can be made into an elegant dinner party pud, especially when accompanied by Lemon-cream-filled Brandy Snaps (see p. 94) or a good ice-cream.

CONTENTS

GOLDEN SYRUP TART *41*

RICH AND QUICK BREAD AND BUTTER PUDDING *42*

RHUBARB WITH ORANGE FUDGE CRUMBLE *43*

BAKED LEMON RICE PUDDING *44*

BAKED DRIED APRICOTS WITH ORANGE AND GINGER *45*

HOT FRESH FRUIT SALAD *46*

PLUM NUT CRUNCH *47*

PINEAPPLE AND PECAN SPICED CAKE *48*

BAKED NUTMEG CUSTARD *49*

APPLES IN BUTTERSCOTCH *50*

TOASTED COCONUT SLICE *51*

BAKED VANILLA SPONGE WITH CHOCOLATE SAUCE *52*

BAKED SPICED PINEAPPLE CAKE *53*

APPLE AND CINNAMON TART *54*

PEAR AND GINGER PUDDING *55*

BAKED APPLES STUFFED WITH DATES *56*

BAKED MINCEMEAT–STUFFED PEARS *57*

PEAR AND BRAMBLE OATMEAL FUDGE CRUMBLE *58*

BANANAS BAKED IN RUM, LIME AND CINNAMON BUTTER *59*

HOT DRIED FRUIT SALAD *60*

GOLDEN SYRUP TART

SERVES

— 6 —

This comes under the category of nursery-type pudding. It can be quickly made using bought shortcrust pastry. You can also make the tart in two stages – cook the pastry case one day and bake the filling the next. My version of this pudding uses crushed cornflakes instead of the more usual white breadcrumbs because the very slight saltiness of the cornflakes counteracts the sweetness of the syrup. You can substitute treacle for the golden syrup if you prefer, but I find that most people prefer the taste of syrup – I do!

INGREDIENTS

350 g (12 oz) shortcrust pastry

FOR THE FILLING:
100 g (4 oz) cornflakes
6 tablespoons golden syrup
50 g (2 oz) melted butter
3 eggs, well beaten

Pre-heat the oven to gas mark 4, 350°F (180°C). Roll out the pastry to line a flan dish approximately 23 cm (9 in) in diameter. Chill the pastry well, then bake blind till the pastry is pale golden, about 20–25 minutes.

Put the cornflakes in a polythene bag and crush with a rolling pin till they are crumb-like. Warm the syrup, butter and beaten eggs together in a pan over gentle heat till the syrup just begins to turn runny. Then stir in the crumbed cornflakes and pour the mixture into the baked pastry case. Put the tart back in the oven for about 20 minutes or till the filling is just set. When you shake the pie gently the filling should barely tremble. Serve cold or warm.

RICH AND QUICK BREAD AND BUTTER PUDDING

SERVES

— 6 —

I have made this often at demonstrations up and down the country, and it is loved even by those who affirm that they loathe the more usual version of bread and butter pud! The malt loaves keep well in the freezer, and can even be sliced from frozen with a good bread knife.

INGREDIENTS

12 slices of malt loaf
450 ml (15 fl oz) single
   cream
Grated rind of half a lemon
Grated rind of half an
   orange
1 egg
2 egg yolks
50 g (2 oz) caster sugar
A grating of nutmeg

Pre-heat the oven to gas mark 4, 350°F (180°C).

Butter the slices of malt loaf. Butter an ovenproof dish and arrange the slices of loaf in the dish. In a bowl beat together all the other ingredients. Pour this mixture over the malt loaf slices and bake till the creamy filling is just set – about 20 minutes. This can be made in advance and rewarmed to serve.

RHUBARB WITH ORANGE FUDGE CRUMBLE

SERVES
— 6–8 —

The tastes of rhubarb and orange complement each other so well. In this pudding, which is meant to be eaten hot but which can be made in advance and reheated without in any way damaging the quality of the pudding, there is not only orange juice in the rhubarb, but the digestive biscuit crumble also has grated orange rind in it. Don't be put off by the inclusion of vanilla essence in the list of ingredients, it goes well with the orange flavour too. A quick tip – the digestives can be crushed to crumbs in seconds using a food processor.

Pre-heat the oven to gas mark 4, 350°F (180°C).

Put the rhubarb, sugar and orange juice into a saucepan (not aluminium, preferably, as the rhubarb is so acidic), cover and cook over a moderate heat till the juices of the rhubarb run into the orange juice, the sugar dissolves, and the pieces of rhubarb become tender. This takes about 15 minutes. Put the rhubarb mixture into an oven-proof dish.

Meanwhile put the butter and sugar into a pan and heat till the butter melts. Stir in the crushed digestives, the vanilla essence and the orange rind and mix thoroughly. Cover the cooked rhubarb with this mixture and bake for 20–25 minutes, till the surface just begins to turn colour. Serve with cream, or Greek yoghurt.

INGREDIENTS

750 g (1½ lb) rhubarb
   (trimmed weight),
150 g (5 oz) soft brown
   sugar
Juice of 2 oranges

FOR THE CRUMBLE:
100 g (4 oz) butter
100 g (4 oz) demerara
   sugar
10 digestive biscuits,
   crushed into crumbs
A few drops of vanilla
   essence
Grated rind of 1 orange

BAKED LEMON RICE PUDDING

SERVES

— 6 —

INGREDIENTS

75 g (3 oz) pudding rice
75 g (3 oz) caster sugar
Grated rind of 1 lemon
1.2 litres (2 pints) full-cream milk
50 g (2 oz) butter, cut into bits

Rice pudding has always been one of my favourite puddings. It was the only item on the menu at school that was really good. For me, a proper rice pudding is a baked rice pudding, and I like it to be lemon-flavoured. If you prefer, you can flavour it with freshly grated nutmeg, or with vanilla. It can be prepared in a minute on your return from work, and then left in the oven to cook until you are ready to eat it. It is useful because it will keep warm endlessly – just turn the heat off in the oven and leave it there till serving time. If you like, stir a handful of raisins into the pudding as it cooks.

Pre-heat the oven to gas mark 4, 350°F (180°C). Butter or oil well an ovenproof dish or soufflé dish. Put the rice, sugar and lemon rind into the dish and pour in the milk. Bake for 1 hour, from time to time forking through the pudding. Then lower the heat to gas mark 3, 325°F (160°C) and cook for a further ¾–1 hour. Dot the butter over the surface.

BAKED DRIED APRICOTS WITH ORANGE AND GINGER

SERVES

— 6 —

This is one of those versatile convenience puddings which can either be made and reheated, or left in a slow cooker all day. It makes a simple finale to a rich dinner or lunch. It can be accompanied by shortbread or ginger biscuits, and any left-over apricots are delicious eaten up for breakfast! It can be served hot or cold, but I prefer it hot or warm.

Pre-heat the oven to gas mark 4, 350°F (180°C).

Put the apricots into an ovenproof dish. Grate the orange rind into the apricots. Squeeze the juice from the oranges and add to the apricots. Add cold water to come about 2.5 cm (1 in) above them. Stir in the chopped ginger and spoon in the ginger syrup. Cover with a lid or foil and bake the apricots for 45 minutes until they are well plumped up. If you have a slow-cooker you can cook them in that over several hours. They really can't be overcooked. Serve hot or cold.

INGREDIENTS

750 g (1½ lb) dried apricots, washed under running water
2 oranges
6 pieces of preserved ginger, chopped
2 tablespoons of the ginger syrup

HOT FRESH FRUIT SALAD

SERVES

—— 6–8 ——

INGREDIENTS

3 dessert apples, Cox's for example
3 pink grapefruit
1 medium to large pineapple
225 g (8 oz) sweet grapes, green or black
½ a 450 g (1 lb) pot of thick honey
4–6 pieces stem ginger (optional), drained

The idea for this recipe was given to me last winter by Olivia Ley, who, with her husband Hugh, is one of the greatest sources of culinary inspiration we know. However, I have taken over the recipe and altered it to my own taste. I have to come clean and warn you that our children, on being fed this for the third time, said firmly but politely that it is *not* one of their favourites. I surmise that it is for adult tastes only!

First prepare the fruit. Peel, core and chop the apples. Slice the skin off the grapefruit and cut into segments by slicing inwards between the skins. Cut the skin off the pineapple and chop the flesh into chunks, discarding the tough 'core'. Halve the grapes and remove the seeds.

Tip the contents of the pot of honey into a saucepan and heat – it will become runny as it gets hot. Add the apples to the hot honey and cook gently for 3 minutes, then add the grapefruit, pineapple and grapes – and the ginger, if you are including it. Heat for 2–3 minutes, then keep in a low temperature oven till you are ready to serve it – it keeps warm very well without spoiling.

PLUM NUT CRUNCH

SERVES
— 6 —

This pudding consists of baked or stewed plums with a crunchy top consisting of crushed walnuts, sesame seeds and oatmeal, bound together with demerara sugar and butter, spiced with a teaspoon of cinnamon. The cinnamon goes with plums so well. Incidentally, cinnamon enhances many other fruits too – try it in dishes using strawberries and raspberries. This dish is very good served with Greek yoghurt, whipped cream, or vanilla ice-cream.

Pre-heat the oven to gas mark 4, 350°F (180°C).

Put the plums and sugar into a saucepan with 3–4 tablespoons of water and stew till the fruit is soft.

As the plums cook they make their own juice so this small amount of water is all that's needed. Discard the plum stones and put the fruit into an ovenproof dish.

In a saucepan melt the butter and add the rest of the ingredients. Stir the mixture and let it cook over a moderate heat for 3–5 minutes, then spoon it over the plums. Smooth the mixture even, and bake for 20–25 minutes, till the top is just beginning to turn toasted-looking. Serve hot or cold.

INGREDIENTS

750 g (1½ lb) plums
75–100 g (3–4 oz) soft brown sugar

FOR THE TOPPING:
100 g (4 oz) butter
75 g (3 oz) pinhead oatmeal or *porridge oats*
100 g (4 oz) demerara sugar
1 teaspoon ground cinnamon
100 g (4 oz) crushed walnuts
50 g (2 oz) sesame seeds

PINEAPPLE AND PECAN SPICED CAKE

SERVES

— 8 —

INGREDIENTS

200 ml (7 fl oz) sunflower oil

225 g (8 oz) caster sugar

225 g (8 oz) self-raising flour, sieved

4 eggs

4 teaspoons ground cinnamon

1 teaspoon vanilla essence

100 g (4 oz) chopped pecan nuts

1 medium-sized pineapple, skin removed and flesh chopped

Pecan nuts are now widely available in this country. They have a buttery texture and, although they bear a resemblance to walnuts, the taste is less pronounced. The spice here is cinnamon, and this cake takes very few minutes to prepare – probably the most laborious part of the preparation is cutting the thick skin off the pineapple, and washing up afterwards!

Pre-heat the oven to gas mark 4, 350°F (180°C). Grease a 25 cm (10 in) cake tin (square or round) and line the base with baking parchment.

In a bowl beat together the oil and caster sugar, then beat in the sieved flour and the eggs, cinnamon, and vanilla essence. Stir in the chopped nuts and the chopped pineapple and pour the cake mixture into the prepared tin. Bake for 1 hour. Let it stand for 10 minutes (in the tin) before serving.

BAKED NUTMEG CUSTARD

SERVES
—— 4–6 ——

This is real nursery food, but so good. It is delicious on its own, or as an accompaniment to fruity dishes, like the Baked Dried Apricots with Orange and Ginger (see p. 45). I love the soft texture of a good baked custard. I don't think you can get this texture without using a combination of whole eggs and yolks. If you use all whole eggs, the texture is much firmer.

(see p. 45)

INGREDIENTS

2 eggs
2 egg yolks
75 g (3 oz) caster sugar
600 ml (1 pint) full-cream milk
A grating of nutmeg

Pre-heat the oven to gas mark 4, 350°F (180°C).

In a bowl beat the eggs well with the yolks and sugar. Heat the milk in a saucepan till it forms a skin. Pour it onto the egg mixture and beat well. Pour through a sieve into a soufflé dish, and grate nutmeg over the surface. Stand in a roasting tin of water and bake for 30 minutes till the custard barely shakes when you gently move the roasting tin. Take it out of the oven, serve warm.

APPLES IN BUTTERSCOTCH

SERVES

— 6 —

INGREDIENTS

6 dessert apples
100 g (4 oz) butter
100 g (4 oz) soft brown
  sugar
3 tablespoons single cream
A few drops of vanilla
  essence

The better the apples used in this dish the better will be the result. My favourite apples for cooking are Cox's, because they have such a definite taste and tartness. My least favourite of all apples (for anything) are Golden Delicious. If Cox's are out of season, Granny Smiths are good too. This dish is very good with vanilla ice-cream, or with Greek yoghurt.

Peel, core and slice the apples into a bowl. Press clingfilm over them. Melt the butter in a saucepan and stir in the soft brown sugar, cream and vanilla essence. Stir till the sugar dissolves and then let the sauce boil gently for at least 5 minutes. Add the sliced apples and continue to cook for 7–10 minutes, gently turning the sliced apples in the sauce from time to time. Keep the apples warm in their sauce till you are ready to serve.

TOASTED COCONUT SLICE

SERVES

— 6 —

This is a vanilla and toasted coconut flavoured cake, and I like to serve it with a simple sauce of black cherry jam warmed with a wine glass of brandy (see p. 121) – or you can use cherry brandy, if you prefer. By dry-toasting the desiccated coconut, in a heavy-based saucepan over heat, it prevents you – if you are like me – from inadvertently char-grilling the coconut and burning it. This is all too easy to do! You can toast the coconut several days before you want to make the cake, if it is more convenient, and store it in a screw-topped jar.

Pre-heat the oven to gas mark 4, 350°F (180°C).

Butter a cake tin measuring approximately 23 cm (9 in) in diameter and line the base of the tin with a disc of baking parchment. Beat the butter and sugar in a bowl until the mixture is very light and fluffy. Then beat in the eggs, one by one, alternating with spoonfuls of the sieved flour. Lastly, beat in the coconut and vanilla essence. Spoon and scrape into the prepared tin, smooth it even and bake for 25 minutes. Serve hot or warm, dusted with a little sieved icing sugar, and with the Cherry Jam Sauce.

INGREDIENTS

100 g (4 oz) butter
100 g (4 oz) caster sugar
4 eggs
175 g (6 oz) self-raising flour, sieved
75 g (3 oz) toasted desiccated coconut
A few drops of vanilla essence
Icing sugar for dusting

BAKED VANILLA SPONGE WITH CHOCOLATE SAUCE

SERVES

—— 6 ——

Butter for greasing
100 g (4 oz) butter
100 g (4 oz) caster sugar
4 eggs
225 g (8 oz) self-raising
  flour, sieved
A few drops of vanilla
  essence
Icing sugar for dusting

FOR THE CHOCOLATE
  SAUCE:

100 g (4 oz) very good
  dark chocolate, broken
  into bits
300 ml (10 fl oz) single
  cream
A few drops of vanilla
  essence

This is a nursery pudding with a difference – the difference is that the hot vanilla-flavoured cake pudding is served with a simple but rich sauce of dark chocolate melted in cream. When accompanied by whipped cream or vanilla ice-cream, this is the sort of pudding people like me dream about!

Pre-heat the oven to gas mark 4, 350°F (180°C).

Rub butter sparingly around the sides and base of a 23 cm (9 in) round cake tin and line the base with a disc of baking parchment. Then beat the 100 g (4 oz) butter and sugar together till the mixture is light and fluffy. Beat in the eggs, one by one, alternately with spoonfuls of the sieved flour. Lastly beat in the vanilla essence. Spoon and scrape this mixture into the prepared tin, smooth even, and bake for about 20–25 minutes. Take the cake out of the oven when it is golden brown and just beginning to come away from the sides of the tin. When slightly cooled, remove from tin and dust with sieved icing sugar.

Meanwhile make the sauce. Put the broken-up chocolate and cream in a saucepan and melt over a gentle heat. Stir in the vanilla essence. Pour into a jug. Serve warm – it thickens as it cools – with the warm cake.

BAKED SPICED PINEAPPLE CAKE

SERVES

— 6 —

The spice in this cake pudding is cardamom. It's a spice which is so fragrant and so good with just about all fruits, but especially, I think, with pineapple. The cake mixture takes about 5 minutes to prepare and about 25 to cook.

Pre-heat the oven to gas mark 4, 350°F (180°C).

Slice the skin off the pineapple using a serrated knife. Cut the skinned pineapple into slices and then into strips, cutting away the central core. Put these strips of pineapple in the bottom of a buttered ovenproof dish. Bash the cardamom pods in a pestle and mortar or in a bowl with the end of a rolling pin. Throw the outer husks away and you will be left with tiny black seeds.

Beat together the butter (or margarine) and sugar till they are pale, soft and fluffy. Beat in the eggs, one at a time, alternating with spoonfuls of the sieved flour. Lastly, beat in the tiny black cardamom seeds. Spoon and scrape this mixture over the sliced pineapple. Smooth it evenly and bake for 25 minutes, till the cake is risen and feels spongy when you press it gently in the middle. Serve hot or warm.

INGREDIENTS

1 medium-sized pineapple
3 whole cardamoms
75 g (3 oz) butter or margarine
75 g (3 oz) caster sugar
3 eggs
175 g (6 oz) self-raising flour, sieved

APPLE AND CINNAMON TART

SERVES
—— 6–8 ——

INGREDIENTS

450 g (1 lb) bought shortcrust pastry

FOR THE FILLING:

4 dessert apples, for example Cox's, peeled, cored and sliced
2 tablespoons lemon juice
2 eggs
1 egg yolk
50 g (2 oz) caster sugar
2 teaspoons ground cinnamon
300 ml (10 fl oz) single cream

If you have bought shortcrust pastry in the freezer, this really doesn't take long to make. The pie can be made several hours in advance and put into a low temperature oven to warm up before serving.

Pre-heat the oven to gas mark 4, 350°F (180°C).

Line a flan dish measuring about 23 cm (9 in) in diameter with the pastry and put it into the freezer for 30 minutes. Then bake till it is golden brown – if your flan dish is metal, this takes about 20 minutes, if it is pot or china, about 30 minutes. Arrange the sliced apples over the cooked pastry and brush with lemon juice to prevent them going brown. Beat together the eggs, yolk, sugar, cinnamon and cream and pour over the apples. Carefully put the flan into the oven for 15–20 minutes, till the filling is just set. Serve warm or cold.

PEAR AND GINGER PUDDING

SERVES
—— 6–8 ——

Pears and ginger are flavours which go together very well. This pudding takes about 5 minutes to make and 35–40 minutes to bake, but it can be made in advance and reheated, or it can be cooking while you eat the main part of your meal. Like all hot puddings, I find it warm and comforting and I like to serve it with cream, Greek yoghurt, vanilla ice-cream, or with custard.

Pre-heat the oven to gas mark 4, 350°F (180°C).

Beat the butter, gradually adding the sugar. Beat well. Sieve the flour with the ginger. Alternating with spoonfuls of the sieved flour, beat in the eggs, one at a time. Lastly beat in the treacle. Peel, core and slice the pears. Butter an ovenproof dish, and put the sliced pears in it. Cover with the mixture, smooth even, and bake for 35–40 minutes. Serve warm or cold, but I much prefer it warm.

INGREDIENTS

100 g (4 oz) butter
100 g (4 oz) soft brown sugar
225 g (8 oz) self-raising flour
3 teaspoons ground ginger
3 eggs
4 tablespoons black treacle
4 pears

BAKED APPLES STUFFED WITH DATES

SERVES

—— 6 ——

INGREDIENTS

6 cooking apples
Grated rind of 1 orange
225 g (8 oz) dried dates,
chopped and stoned
6 teaspoons soft brown
sugar
50 g (2 oz) butter
Juice of 1 orange
150 ml (5 fl oz) water

I like cooking mostly with eating apples, but for apples which are to be stuffed, you really do need to use cookers. The tartness of the cooked apple and its soft texture, contrast well with the orange and date filling. These take about 2 minutes to prepare and about 15 to cook. They keep warm well and can be served either with Greek yoghurt, cream or ice-cream or – best of all – custard.

Pre-heat the oven to gas mark 4, 350°F (180°C).

Wash the apples, core them, and score round the equator of each. This helps to prevent them from bursting during their baking. Mix the grated orange rind with the chopped dates, and add the sugar. Divide this date mixture between the 6 apples. stuffing it down the hole left by the core. Put the apples into a roasting tin or an ovenproof dish, cut the butter into 6 even bits and put one on top of each stuffed apple. Pour the orange juice and water into the tin or dish. Cover the apples with a piece of greaseproof paper and bake for 15 minutes, or until the apples feel soft when you stick a fork gently into the middle of one. Serve immediately.

BAKED MINCEMEAT-STUFFED PEARS

SERVES
— 6 —

This is simplicity itself. Choose large and juicy pears. I like to leave the skins on but you can peel them if you prefer. I find a potato peeler the quickest and simplest way of peeling them. Brushing the pear halves with lemon juice helps to prevent them from discolouring and means that you can do this and leave the dish ready to pop into the oven as you sit down to the main course. The pears are delicious with custard but you can serve them with cream, ice-cream or Greek yoghurt.

INGREDIENTS

6 large, ripe pears
12 generous teaspoons
bought mincemeat
Juice of 1 orange
150 ml (5 fl oz) water

Pre-heat the oven to gas mark 4, 350°F (180°C).

Cut each pear in half, top to bottom, and scoop out the core. Put the pear halves, cut side up, into a roasting tin or ovenproof dish. Spoon the mincemeat, 1 teaspoon per pear half, into the dent left by the core. Pour the orange juice and water around the pears, cover the top with a piece of greaseproof paper and bake for 10 minutes. Serve immediately.

PEAR AND BRAMBLE OATMEAL FUDGE CRUMBLE

SERVES

—— 6–8 ——

INGREDIENTS

3 large pears
1 tablespoon lemon juice
450 g (1 lb) blackberries,
    fresh or frozen
2–3 tablespoons granulated
    sugar

FOR THE CRUMBLE:
100 g (4 oz) butter
2 teaspoons ground
    cinnamon
175 g (6 oz) pinhead
    oatmeal or porridge oats
100 g (4 oz) demerara
    sugar
½ teaspoon vanilla essence

This easy and delicious crumble-with-a-difference can be served with whipped cream, Greek yoghurt, or with vanilla ice-cream. If you serve it with the latter, the crumble is best served warm, otherwise it is equally good served warm or cold. It reheats very well.

Pre-heat the oven to gas mark 4, 350°F (180°C). Peel, core and chop the pears and toss in the lemon juice.

Put the blackberries and chopped pears into an oven-proof dish and fork the sugar through them. To make the crumble, melt the butter in saucepan and stir in the cinnamon, oatmeal, demerara sugar and vanilla, mixing all together well. Spoon this evenly over the blackberries and pears, and bake for 45–50 minutes. Serve hot or cold.

BANANAS BAKED IN RUM, LIME AND CINNAMON BUTTER

SERVES
— 6 —

This takes about 1 minute to assemble, 10 to bake. The flavoured rum butter can be made and kept in the fridge for up to 3 weeks. It's quite useful to have two or three times the amount in the fridge ready for this quick pudding. If you do store this butter in the fridge it will become hard, so remember to take it out of the fridge and into room temperature for an hour or so before trying to spread it over the bananas.

Pre-heat the oven to gas mark 4, 350°F (180°C).

Beat the butter, gradually adding the sugar and beating till the mixture is soft and fluffy. Then beat in the rum, a little at a time, the grated lime and the cinnamon.

Peel the bananas, and put them into an ovenproof dish, spread or dot the flavoured butter over them, and bake for 10 minutes. Serve immediately.

INGREDIENTS

6 medium to large bananas

FOR THE BUTTER:
75 g (3 oz) butter, preferably unsalted
75 g (3 oz) soft brown sugar
3 tablespoons rum
Grated rind of lime
1–2 teaspoons ground cinnamon

HOT DRIED FRUIT SALAD

SERVES

—— 6 ——

1 Lapsang Souchong
  teabag
750 g (1½ lb) mixed dried
  fruit, larger fruit cut in
  half
2 tablespoons thick honey
Juice of 1 lemon

You can buy bags of mixed dried fruits in healthfood shops and delicatessens, or you can choose your favourite individual dried fruits and mix them up yourself. Personally, I'm not so keen on dried figs which to me are too reminiscent of syrup of figs! I love the smoky taste of Lapsang Souchong tea, and I think that its flavour and the lemon juice and honey in the recipe all complement each other very well. As with the Baked Dried Apricots (see p. 45), any left-over Hot Dried Fruit Salad makes a delicious breakfast, especially when accompanied by a spoonful or two of Greek or natural yoghurt.

Pre-heat the oven to gas mark 4, 350°F (180°C).

Boil a kettle and make about 900 ml (1½ pints) of tea using the Lapsang teabag. After two or three minutes' infusing time, fish out the teabag. Put the dried fruits into an ovenproof dish and pour the tea over the fruits. Stir in the honey and the lemon juice. Cover the dish and bake for 1 hour or leave it in a slow cooker for several hours. You can leave the dish in a low temperature oven for ages, this really cannot overcook. Serve hot or cold.

FROZEN PUDDINGS

These really are the quickest of all puddings – they need only to be taken out of the freezer. Admittedly some of them need to come out half an hour or so before they are to be eaten, but then you are going to eat a main course first anyway so they can be sitting at room temperature during that time. Dishes in this chapter which benefit from this spell of time out of the freezer before being eaten are the water ices (or sorbets), and the ice-cream cakes (see p. 71). However, recipes which have any liqueurs or spirits in them, like the Iced Lemon and Honey Creams (see p. 80), which contain brandy, or the Irish Coffee Liqueur Creams (see p. 78), can be eaten direct from the freezer – the spirit prevents them from freezing rock-hard.

I do realize that all these frozen puddings need to be made at some point, but you can choose the time which is convenient for you and which will fit into your routine. None of the recipes is lengthy and time-consuming. In the case of the water ices which need to be blended in a food processor three times during their freezing time, this can be done over several days, rather than fitted into one particular day. They are blended from the totally frozen state and refrozen. It doesn't matter a bit if they thaw out a little because there is no cream involved to make refreezing at all harmful.

CONTENTS

FUDGE AND PECAN NUT ICE-CREAM *63*

HONEY, BANANA AND YOGHURT ICE-CREAM *64*

VANILLA AND MINT CHIP ICE-CREAM *65*

MANGO AND ORANGE WATER ICE *66*

TWO ICE-CREAM CAKES

VICTORIA SPONGE *72*

MERINGUE CAKE *73*

LEMON AND COINTREAU WATER ICE–FILLED

ORANGE SHELLS *74*

LEMON AND BLACKCURRANT WATER ICE *75*

PINEAPPLE AND LEMON WATER ICE *76*

MELON AND LAPSANG SOUCHONG TEA

WATER ICE *77*

IRISH COFFEE LIQUEUR CREAMS *78*

VANILLA ICE AND MERINGUE FLAMBÉ *79*

ICED LEMON AND HONEY CREAMS *80*

CRANBERRY AND ORANGE WATER ICE *81*

*F*UDGE AND PECAN NUT ICE-CREAM

SERVES

— 6 —

This is simplicity itself if you have any left-over Fudge Sauce (see p. 119). The idea of stirring it into vanilla ice-cream, which is all this recipe is about, originated with Louise, who was my cousin Nick's wife. Then I thought of adding a few chopped pecan nuts and it seemed even better. You can, of course, leave out the nuts if you don't like them, or if you don't have any.

INGREDIENTS

600 ml (1 pint) vanilla ice-cream
50–75 g (2–3 oz) pecan nuts, chopped
½ quantity Fudge sauce (see p. 119)

Leave the ice-cream at room temperature for about 15 minutes. This softens it slightly. Mix in the chopped nuts and then beat the fudge sauce into the ice-cream, leaving it streaky – don't try to mix it in thoroughly. Refreeze in the ice-cream container.

HONEY, BANANA AND YOGHURT ICE-CREAM

S E R V E S
—— 6–8 ——

3 bananas
2 tablespoons honey, thick
* or runny*
1 teaspoon ground
* cinnamon*
600 ml (1 pint) natural
* yoghurt*

My daughter first introduced me to the combination of banana and yoghurt frozen as an ice-cream but, on experimenting with the combination, we both thought that it could do with a bit of sweetener so we opted for honey. Then I thought a touch of cinnamon might embellish it still further. This is the result. It's quick to make, healthy to eat, and in the strawberry season you can add strawberries to the mixture, puréed with the bananas – the two fruits go together extremely well. Using a Greek yoghurt also makes it even nicer if slightly less healthy!

Liquidize or process the bananas (without their skins!) with the honey and cinnamon. When they are smooth, stir them into the yoghurt. Freeze in a solid, polythene container. After several hours, whisk the semi-frozen mixture – this is easiest done with a hand-held electric whisk. Put back into the freezer and take out half an hour before serving.

VANILLA AND MINT CHIP ICE-CREAM

SERVES

—— 4–6 ——

This recipe is almost embarrassingly simple – but it's so good I just had to include it here! As it is very high on my children's list of favourite puddings, I think you'll like it too.

The chocolate mints which work best are mint matchsticks and solid, round chocolates with mint chips. My favourite chocolates for this recipe are Elizabeth Shaw dark chocolate Mint Crisps.

Take the ice-cream out of the freezer and allow it to thaw at room temperature for 15 minutes. In a food processor, whiz the chocolates briefly till they are crumb-like. Scrape them all out of the processor and into the ice-cream. Mix them in as best you can. Refreeze the ice-cream and serve.

INGREDIENTS

600 ml (1 pint) good quality vanilla ice-cream
100 g (4 oz) crisp mint chocolates

MANGO AND ORANGE WATER ICE

SERVES

—— 6 ——

INGREDIENTS

3 mangoes
600 ml (1 pint) fresh
orange juice
Slices of mango and orange
to serve (optional)

You can buy mangoes now in most large supermarkets. Press them gently – they should be soft (but not squishy) to be ripe. The taste of mango and orange is so good together, and this water ice is simplicity itself to make.

With a sharp knife pare the skin off the mangoes. Slice the mango flesh from the stones, and put it into a food processor. Blend with the orange juice. Freeze in a solid, polythene container.

Chip the frozen mango and orange water ice into a food processor and blend till smooth. Refreeze. Repeat this process at least twice more – the texture will become soft and the water ice will increase in volume. It will now also be the right consistency able to be spooned straight from the freezer. If you like, serve accompanied by slices of mango and oranges.

Opposite: PLUM NUT CRUNCH (*page 47*)

Overleaf: BAKED NUTMEG CUSTARD (*page 49*)
BAKED DRIED APRICOTS WITH ORANGE AND GINGER (*page 45*)

TWO ICE-CREAM CAKES

These must be the easiest type of celebration cakes, because the cakes or meringues can be made when it's convenient for you, rather than on the day itself. When you need them you just thaw and fill them with vanilla ice-cream. It is useful to have two Victoria sponges in your freezer because they thaw quickly – about 30 minutes at room temperature – and can then also be filled with jam, and either whipped cream or vanilla butter cream for an emergency tea. The only point I would make is to advise you not to thaw them in a microwave because I don't think that any baked goods microwave well – it seems to take the moisture out of them. For the meringue cake you don't need to thaw the meringue before filling it with vanilla ice-cream. I like to serve either cake accompanied by a sauce of puréed strawberries or raspberries like Fruit Sauce (see p. 120).

Preceding page: BAKED VANILLA SPONGE WITH CHOCOLATE SAUCE (*page 52*)

Opposite: APPLE AND CINNAMON TART (*page 54*)

VICTORIA SPONGE

SERVES

—— 6–8 ——

INGREDIENTS

175 g (6 oz) butter
175 g (6 oz) caster sugar
3 eggs
175 g (6 oz) self-raising
  flour, sieved
A few drops of vanilla
  essence

Pre-heat the oven to gas mark 4, 350°F (180°C). Butter two 18 cm (7 in) sandwich cake tins and line the base of each with a disc of baking parchment.

In a bowl beat the butter well, gradually adding the caster sugar. Beat till fluffy. Beat in the eggs one by one, alternating with spoonfuls of the sieved flour. Lastly, beat in the vanilla essence. Divide the mixture between the prepared tins, smooth even, and bake for 25–30 minutes till the cakes are golden brown and just beginning to come away from the sides of their tins. Leave in their tins for about half a minute, then turn out to cool on a wire rack. When they are quite cold, wrap each well in foil or clingfilm, label and freeze until required.

MERINGUE CAKE

SERVES

—— 6–8 ——

Pre-heat the oven to gas mark 4, 350°F (180°C). Line a baking tray with a piece of baking parchment and, using an 18 cm (7 in) plate as a template, draw two circles on it.

Whisk the whites and salt till they are very stiff. Then, still whisking, add the sugar a spoonful at a time, whisking till the sugar is all incorporated. Divide the mixture between the two marked circles, and smooth evenly. Bake for 2½–3 hours.

When they lift off the paper quite easily, the meringues are cooked. Cool them on a wire rack. When they are quite cold, pack them carefully in a tin or solid polythene container and freeze until needed.

INGREDIENTS

3 egg whites
A pinch of salt
175 g (6 oz) caster sugar

LEMON AND COINTREAU WATER ICE-FILLED ORANGE SHELLS

SERVES

—— 6 ——

900 ml (1½ pints) water
350 g (12 oz) granulated
*   sugar*
Pared rind and juice of 2
*   lemons*
150 ml (5 fl oz) Cointreau
6 oranges

Although the preparation of the orange shells takes a bit of time, you can make this in stages at your convenience by preparing the oranges and leaving them cut side down on kitchen paper over a day or even two. The water ice is quickly spooned into the shells to serve, and they do look pretty for a special occasion. Of course, you can just eat the water ice without bothering with the shells! A final tip before beginning: I use a potato peeler to pare lemon rind, it avoids slicing any bitter white pith with the rind.

Put the water into a saucepan with the sugar and pared lemon rind. Over a moderate heat stir occasionally till the sugar dissolves completely, then boil the liquid fast for 5 minutes. Take the pan off the heat and remove the strips of lemon rind, and stir in the lemon juice. Cool. Stir the Cointreau into the lemon syrup and pour into a solid container and freeze.

Chip the frozen water ice into a food processor and blend. Refreeze. Repeat twice more.

To prepare the oranges, slice the top off each one. With a spoon, scoop out all the flesh. Spoon the water ice into the orange shells – if you like you can replace the tops. Refreeze. Serve them straight from the freezer. The water ice will be spoonable from frozen.

LEMON AND BLACKCURRANT WATER ICE

SERVES

— 6 —

L emon enhances the flavour of many summer and autumn fruits, blackcurrants among them. As with all water ices, providing this is whizzed in a food processor and refrozen at least three times the end result will be spoonable straight from the freezer – truly an ideal instant pud.

Put the blackcurrants (don't bother to top and tail them, they will be liquidized and sieved later) into a saucepan with 150 ml (5 fl oz) water and cook gently till they are soft. Cool, liquidize and sieve the purée. This can be done at your convenience a day or two before you make the water ice and kept in the fridge.

Put 600 ml (1 pint) water, the granulated sugar and the pared lemon rind into a saucepan over moderate heat and stir occasionally till the sugar dissolves completely. Then boil the liquid fast for 5 minutes. Take the pan off the heat and add the lemon juice. Fish out the strips of lemon peel and stir in the blackcurrant purée. Taste to see if you think it is sweet enough – if you would like to add more sugar stir in a tablespoonful or two of sieved icing sugar. Freeze the mixture in a solid, polythene container.

When frozen chip the water ice into a food processor and whiz. Return it to the container and refreeze. Repeat this at least twice more.

INGREDIENTS

350 g (12 oz) blackcurrants
150 ml (5 fl oz) water
600 ml (1 pint) water
225 g (8 oz) granulated sugar
Pared rind and juice of 1 lemon
2 tablespoons icing sugar (optional)

PINEAPPLE AND LEMON WATER ICE

SERVES
— 6 —

INGREDIENTS

600 ml (1 pint) cold water
225 g (8 oz) granulated sugar
Pared rind and juice of 1 lemon
1 medium-sized pineapple, peeled and cut into chunks

The lemon emphasizes the flavour of the pineapple. This is a refreshing and delicious pud, ideal to round off a meal which has rather rich preceding courses. The more often you manage to whiz the frozen water ice in a food processor, the easier it will be to spoon it from its container and the less time it will need at room temperature – the whizzing makes such a soft and smooth-textured water ice.

Measure the water into a saucepan and add the sugar and the lemon rind. Over a gentle heat dissolve the sugar in the water – don't let it boil until the sugar has dissolved completely. Then boil fast for 5 minutes. Take the saucepan off the heat, stir in the lemon juice and leave to cool.

Meanwhile, whiz the pineapple flesh in a processor. Fish the bits of lemon peel out of the syrup and stir the puréed pineapple into the syrup. Freeze in a solid polythene container. Two or three times, chisel the frozen water ice into the processor and whiz. Then refreeze each time.

MELON AND LAPSANG SOUCHONG TEA WATER ICE

SERVES
— 6 —

The smoky taste of the tea in this recipe and the cool taste of the melon combine to make a delicate, different and delicious water ice. As with anything you cook, it will be as good as the melon with which you make it. You can choose a good melon by gently pressing the end – it should give slightly. A good, ripe melon should also have a sweet, fragrant smell. For this recipe Charentais or Ogen melons are good, partly because I like the pale coral-coloured flesh.

INGREDIENTS

1 ripe melon
600 ml (1 pint) water
1 Lapsang Souchong teabag
225 g (8 oz) granulated sugar
Pared rind and juice of 1 lemon

First prepare the melon by discarding the seeds, scooping out the flesh and puréeing it in a food processor.

Put the water into a saucepan and bring to the boil. When it boils, dip the teabag into the water and take the pan off the heat. Leave to infuse for 3–5 minutes. Then take out the teabag, add the sugar and pared lemon rind to the saucepan, and replace on the heat. Don't let the water boil again till the sugar has dissolved completely, then bring to the boil and boil fast for 5 minutes. Take the saucepan off the heat and add the lemon juice. Leave to cool. Then fish out the strips of lemon peel and stir in the melon purée. Pour into a solid polythene container and freeze.

When frozen scoop the water ice into a food processor and whiz till smooth. Refreeze. Repeat this whizzing process at least twice more. After three processings the water ice is so smooth that you can spoon it straight from the freezer.

*I*RISH COFFEE LIQUEUR CREAMS

FILLS 6
LARGE RAMEKINS

INGREDIENTS

2 tablespoons thick honey
3 egg yolks
1 teaspoon instant coffee
granules dissolved in 2
tablespoons boiling water
300 ml (10 fl oz) double
cream
3 tablespoons Bailey's Irish
Cream Liqueur
Small piece of dark
chocolate to decorate

These are so convenient because they can be eaten straight from the freezer. I like to accompany them with chocolate-flavoured biscuits of some sort, as I love the tastes of coffee and chocolate together.

Put the honey into a saucepan. (If you dip the tablespoon in very hot water first, then the honey will slip easily off the spoon.) Heat the honey till it is runny and smoky. Whisk the egg yolks in a bowl, pouring on the hot honey in a steady stream and whisking continuously. Whisk till you have a thick pale mixture. Whisk in the instant coffee.

In a separate bowl whip the cream with the liqueur. Fold together the two mixtures, and divide between the ramekins. Freeze. If you like, as a garnish, you can shave some dark chocolate over the surface of each ramekin, using a potato peeler to do the job quickly.

*V*ANILLA ICE AND MERINGUE FLAMBÉ

S E R V E S

—— 6 ——

This is like Baked Alaska without the sponge base. In many ways I see no need for the sponge base – I never like to consume unnecessary calories, and would much rather eat more of the ice-cream and meringue. This is such a convenient pud, because you can put the ice-cream into an ovenproof dish, make the meringue mixture and cover the ice-cream with it completely – right up to the sides of the dish – and freeze the pudding (uncovered) up to a week ahead. Then, just before you need it you just pop it into a hot oven for 15 minutes. I like to sprinkle granulated sugar over the meringue (and flaked almonds, too, if you like) and ignite a small amount of brandy to pour over the pudding before bringing the dish to the table. If you like, you can use chocolate ice-cream and stud the meringue with slivers of ginger, instead of the vanilla ice-cream and flaked almonds.

INGREDIENTS

4 large egg whites
225 g (8 oz) caster sugar
600 ml (1 pint) vanilla
* ice-cream*
1 tablespoon granulated
* sugar*
2 oz flaked almonds
* (optional)*
150 ml (5 fl oz) brandy

Pre-heat the oven to gas mark 6, 400°F (200°C).

Whisk the egg whites till they are stiff, then, whisking continuously, add the caster sugar a spoonful at a time, till it is all incorporated.

Put the ice-cream into an ovenproof serving dish and cover with the meringue mixture right to the edges of the dish. Put it into the freezer. When you are almost ready to serve it, put the dish straight from the freezer into the oven for 15 minutes. 5 minutes before the end of cooking time, sprinkle the granulated sugar (and flaked almonds, if using) over the meringue before putting it back into the oven. Just before you bring it to the table, gently warm the brandy in a small saucepan and ignite it. Pour this over the meringue, and serve immediately.

*I*CED LEMON
AND HONEY CREAMS

FILLS 6 LARGE
OR 8 SMALL RAMEKINS

INGREDIENTS

3 tablespoons thick honey
3 egg yolks
300 ml (10 fl oz) double
cream
3 tablespoons brandy
1 lemon

This is an invaluable recipe because the brandy in the recipe means it never freezes rock solid and so the creams can be eaten the minute they are out of the freezer.

Heat the honey in a small saucepan. Beat the yolks till thick then, still beating, add the hot honey in a steady trickle till it is absorbed and the mixture is thick and pale. Whip the cream, gradually adding the brandy, till it is about the same consistency as the yolks mixture – this makes them easier to fold together. Grate the rind of the lemon into the whipped cream, fold the two mixtures together thoroughly, and pour into the ramekins. Put the ramekins on a tray and freeze. When they are frozen take the ramekins out of the freezer and cover each with clingfilm, then put them back in the freezer until required.

CRANBERRY AND ORANGE WATER ICE

SERVES

—— 6–8 ——

Fresh cranberries are very widely available these days – several years ago we could only buy frozen cranberries. The one thing to remember about fresh cranberries is to simmer them gently till they are soft before you add any sugar to them. Somehow, if you add sugar to the saucepan with the uncooked cranberries the skins of the berries remain tough. The flavours of cranberry and orange are very complementary to one another and this water ice makes a refreshing end to a rich meal during the winter-time, when cranberries are in the shops.

INGREDIENTS

450 g (1 lb) cranberries
150 ml (5 fl oz) fresh orange juice
600 ml (1 pint) water
225 g (8 oz) granulated sugar
Pared rind of 1 lemon
Pared rind of 1 orange

Put the cranberries into a saucepan with the orange juice and cover. Simmer very gently till the berries are soft when you press them against the side of the saucepan with the back of a wooden spoon. Cool, liquidize and, to get a really smooth purée, sieve the liquidized cranberries.

While the cranberries are cooking, measure the pint of water into a saucepan and add the granulated sugar and the pared lemon and orange rind. Over a moderate heat stir occasionally till the sugar dissolves completely, then let the liquid come to a fast boil. Boil for 5 minutes. Take the pan off the heat, fish out the rinds and stir in the puréed berries. Cool and freeze in a solid, polythene container.

When frozen scoop the water ice into a food processor and whiz. Refreeze. Repeat this process twice. Each time you do this, the mixture will become softer in texture, so that after three processings it will be spoonable straight from the freezer.

QUICK PUDDINGS
FOR ENTERTAINING

The recipes in this chapter are all suitable for parties, of a grand or an informal nature. To qualify for being thought elegant enough a pud to be served to guests doesn't mean that cream is involved in every single recipe. The Fresh Peaches or Nectarines with Raspberry Sauce (see p. 95), for example, are a calorie watcher's delight, so too would be the Lychees in Crème de Menthe (see p. 112) and the Fresh Orange and Chopped Strawberry Jelly (see p. 93). But cream does feature in most of the recipes and, for a special occasion whether of a minor or major type, surely cream is permitted once in a while? But what all these recipes have in common, as ever, is that they are exceptionally quick to make, and therefore make for extra convenient entertaining. I urge you to try the Chocolate Bread Cream (see p. 113), an unlikely name for such a delicious pudding, I agree. When I first ate it I couldn't guess the ingredients, and was bowled over to discover that breadcrumbs featured largely. That particular recipe, whilst taking literally minutes to make, needs to be made a day in advance, so all you need to do before serving it is to take the dish out of the fridge and remove the covering clingfilm – and wait for your guests to exclaim with glee!

CONTENTS

CHERRY YOGHURT CREAM WITH CRUNCHY TOP *86*

EDWARDIAN CREAM *87*

STRAWBERRY AND ALMOND CREAM *88*

GRAPE AND LEMON BRULÉE *89*

LYCHEE PARFAIT *90*

LEMON RICE CREAM *91*

BANANA-FILLED PANCAKES WITH FUDGE SAUCE *92*

FRESH ORANGE AND CHOPPED STRAWBERRY JELLY *93*

LEMON CREAM-FILLED BRANDY SNAPS *94*

FRESH PEACHES OR NECTARINES WITH RASPBERRY SAUCE *95*

LEMON AND GINGER SYLLABUB *96*

COFFEE JELLY WITH AMARETTI CREAM *97*

CHOCOLATE OATMEAL BISCUIT CREAM *98*

CHOCOLATE MERINGUE CAKE *99*

PEARS IN CHOCOLATE MOUSSE *100*

APRICOT FOOL WITH MARRONS GLACÉS *101*

ATHOLL BROSE *102*

QUICK SHERRY TRIFLE *105*

RASPBERRY CREAM BRULÉE *106*

CHOCOLATE BRANDY SYLLABUB *107*

CARAMEL BANANA CREAM *108*

PEARS WITH BUTTERSCOTCH SAUCE *109*

THE BEST UNCOOKED CHOCOLATE FUDGE CAKE *110*

DIGESTIVE AND CINNAMON PIE WITH

BLACKBERRY FILLING *111*

CONTENTS

LYCHES IN CRÈME DE MENTHE *112*

CHOCOLATE BREAD CREAM *113*

MELITA'S LEMON PUDDING *114*

ORANGE, RHUBARB AND GINGER CREAM *115*

GINGER COFFEE CREAM *116*

BLACKCURRANT WHIP *117*

CHERRY YOGHURT CREAM WITH CRUNCHY TOP

SERVES
— 4 —

INGREDIENTS

50 g (2 oz) sesame seeds
25 g (1 oz) pinhead
  oatmeal or porridge oats
225 g (8 oz) cherries,
  stoned
300 ml (10 fl oz) Greek
  yoghurt
300 ml (10 fl oz) double
  cream, whipped
50 g (2 oz) demerara sugar

This is a very quick pudding to make but benefits from being made several hours in advance. It only takes two minutes to stone the cherries if you have a cherry stoner, so it may be worth investing in one.

The toasted sesame seeds and pinhead oatmeal can be dry-fried days ahead and kept in a screw-topped jar before being mixed with the demerara sugar.

Start by putting the sesame seeds and pinhead oatmeal into a saucepan and heating over a moderate heat, shaking the pan so that the oatmeal and seeds brown evenly. When they are pale golden brown, remove from the heat and cool.

Divide the stoned cherries between individual glasses or dishes. Fold together the yoghurt and cream. Spoon this evenly over the cherries. Mix the oatmeal and sesame seeds with the demerara sugar and scatter over each serving. Leave to sit for as long as possible before serving so the flavours have time to mingle.

EDWARDIAN CREAM

SERVES

—— 4–6 ——

This pudding looks particularly pretty when it's served in a glass bowl or in individual glasses. The two-tone effect of the creamy base contrasts well with the jewel-like, puréed fruit top.

Liquidize the fruit with the sugar until a purée is formed. Sieve the purée to remove all the pips.

Beat together the butter and cream cheese until they are light and fluffy. Still beating, add the granulated sugar, lemon juice and vanilla essence.

Spoon the mixture into the base of a serving dish or into the individual dishes and pour over the fruit purée.

INGREDIENTS

FOR THE FRUIT PURÉE:
450 g (1 lb) raspberries or strawberries or other soft fruit
50 g (2 oz) icing sugar

100 g (4 oz) unsalted butter
225 g (8 oz) cream cheese
75 g (3 oz) granulated sugar
2 teaspoons lemon juice
1 teaspoon vanilla essence

STRAWBERRY AND ALMOND CREAM

SERVES
—— 4 ——

450 g (1 lb) strawberries, hulled and cut in half
50 g (2 oz) flaked almonds
300 ml (10 fl oz) double cream
a few drops of almond essence or 1 tablespoon almond liqueur
caster sugar to taste
4 good strawberries for garnishing

The toasted, flaked almonds double up both as a flavour contrast as well as a texture contrast in this delicious, quick and easy dessert.

Divide the hulled and halved strawberries between four serving bowls or glasses.

Toast the flaked almonds by dry-frying them in a pan, shaking the pan as they cook. Cool the golden brown almonds by tipping them onto a plate.

Meanwhile, whip the cream with the almond essence or liqueur, and caster sugar, to your taste.

Spoon into the serving dish or individual dishes and scatter over the toasted almonds. Garnish with remaining strawberries.

GRAPE AND LEMON BRULÉE

SERVES

— 4 —

This can be made several hours in advance and finished just before serving. The grated lemon in the whipped cream gives just the right amount of bite to the flavour and contrasts deliciously with the crunchy sugar top.

Cut each grape in half and discard any pips. Divide the grape halves between the ramekins.

Whip the cream together with the egg white until stiff. Fold in the grated lemon rind using a spoon.

Divide the cream evenly between the ramekins, smoothing the surfaces. At this point you can cover the ramekins with clingfilm and leave them in the fridge.

To finish the brulée, heat the grill until it is very hot. Cover the surface of each ramekin with a tablespoon of granulated sugar and grill until the sugar melts and just begins to caramelize. Let them cool slightly before serving.

INGREDIENTS

225 g (8 oz) grapes, green or black
300 ml (10 fl oz) double cream
1 large egg white
grated rind of 1 well-washed (and dried) lemon
4 tablespoons granulated sugar

LYCHEE PARFAIT

SERVES
—— 6 ——

1 × 425 g (15 oz) tin of lychees
1 sachet gelatine
300 ml (10 fl oz) double cream
2 egg whites

This can be made in minutes providing you have a tin of lychees in the store-cupboard. They have a delicious yet delicate flavour, and because the juice from the tin is used in the recipe there is no need for any extra sugar – even for those who have a tooth as sweet as mine! Decorate the parfait, if you like, with grated dark chocolate, or with slivers of preserved ginger. The dish can be made up to two days in advance and kept, covered, in the fridge.

Pour about 3 tablespoons of the juice from the tin of lychees into a small saucepan, and sprinkle the contents of the sachet of gelatine into the liquid – it will sponge up. Over a gentle heat shake the pan till the granules of gelatine dissolve completely. Take the pan off the heat and stir in the rest of the juice from the tin. Leave to cool completely, which will only be a minute or two as the liquid from the tin cools the gelatine liquid rapidly.

Meanwhile whip the cream. Chop the lychees in half and fold them into the whipped cream. When the juice and gelatine liquid begins to jellify as it cools, fold that into the cream and lychees. Leave in the fridge for a few minutes till it is beginning to set.

Lastly, whisk the egg whites till they are very stiff and hold their shape when the whisk lifts them in peaks and, with a large metal spoon, fold them quickly and thoroughly through the lychee mixture. Turn into a glass or china serving bowl and serve.

LEMON RICE CREAM

SERVES

—— 6–8 ——

INGREDIENTS

50 g (2 oz) pudding rice
600 ml (1 pint) milk
50 g (2 oz) caster sugar
Pared rind of half a lemon
300 ml (10 fl oz) double
  cream, lightly whipped
Grated rind of half a lemon
1 tablespoon icing sugar
  (optional)

When I was small I remember my mother making a cold rice pudding for dinner parties. Much as I loved straightforward rice pudding myself (and there is a recipe in the Hot Puddings chapter, see p. 44, for one) I do realize that so far this doesn't sound much like dinner party-type food. But when I tell you that the rice is lemon-flavoured and has whipped cream folded into it I'm sure you'll agree that this sounds much more the thing. I've asked my mother, but she can't remember where she got the recipe from, so last summer we just made it for our hotel guests as we like it. It is quite delicious served with a compote of raspberries and black-currants or stewed or baked fruit – as always, the lemony taste goes so very well with the fruits.

Put the rice, milk, sugar and pared lemon rind into a saucepan and cook over a gentle heat, with the milk barely simmering, till the rice is soft. Take the pan off the heat, and leave to cool completely. When the rice is cold, fold the lightly whipped cream into the rice – fish out the pared rind, and stir in the grated lemon rind. Taste and if it isn't sweet enough for you carefully sieve in the icing sugar. Spoon and scrape into a serving dish.

BANANA-FILLED PANCAKES WITH FUDGE SAUCE

SERVES

—— 6 ——

12 small to medium-sized bananas
12 bought crêpes or pancakes

FOR THE SAUCE:
175 g (6 oz) butter, preferably unsalted
175 g (6 oz) soft light or dark brown sugar
150 ml (5 fl oz) double cream
½ teaspoon vanilla essence

The fudge sauce recipe is mine, the idea for this dish is not. I always like to give credit where it's due. A great friend of ours, Ann Shuttleworth, triumphantly told me of this discovery of hers, and how her three boys (now aged 16, 14 and 12!) love it. I do feel that this is proof of how good it is! I serve them warm with vanilla ice-cream. You can buy ready-made plain pancakes, which is what I suggest if you are in a hurry. If you put the dish together in the morning, reheat it before serving by putting it into a cool oven as you start dinner or lunch.

Peel each banana and slice. Divide between the pancakes. Roll each pancake up and lay them in an ovenproof dish. Meanwhile put the fudge sauce ingredients into a saucepan, melt and dissolve the butter and sugar, stirring, then let the sauce bubble for 3–5 minutes. Pour the fudge sauce over the pancakes and keep warm in a low temperature oven until serving.

*F*RESH ORANGE AND CHOPPED STRAWBERRY JELLY

S E R V E S
—— 6–8 ——

I've always loved anything jellied, although sweet rather than savoury jelly is my preference. A dessert like this one, accompanied by some crisp biscuits, makes a good fresh ending to a summer meal – although these days strawberries are available from differing parts of the world all year round. It is nicest made with freshly squeezed orange juice (bought from the supermarket, of course!). You can, if you wish, make the jelly in a terrine or loaf tin rather than a bowl or individual glasses. To serve, dip the tin in hot water and turn out to slice. (You will need an extra half-sachet of gelatine to the same amount of water to make a terrine.)

INGREDIENTS

300 ml (10 fl oz) cold water
1 sachet gelatine
2 tablespoons lemon juice
600 ml (1 pint) freshly squeezed orange juice
450 g (1 lb) strawberries, hulled and chopped

Measure the cold water into a pan and sprinkle in the gelatine. Add the lemon juice and heat gently till the gelatine granules have dissolved completely, but take care not to let it boil. Stir this mixture into the orange juice and put it into a serving bowl. Stir in the chopped strawberries and put the bowl in the fridge. Leave to set.

LEMON CREAM-FILLED BRANDY SNAPS

SERVES

—— 6 ——

300 ml (10 fl oz) double cream
2 tablespoons runny honey
Grated rind and juice of 1 lemon
12 brandy snaps

Brandy snaps are delicious, and one of the most useful stand-bys to have in a store-cupboard for emergencies. But with a fairly small amount of extra effort a cream filling can make brandy snaps more special. This filling contains lemon and honey which both enhance the flavour of the brandy snaps. I don't know why the mention of a piping bag makes some people groan because it is honestly so very much easier and quicker to fill things like éclairs, profiteroles, and these brandy snaps using a piping bag with a wide, plain nozzle than if you try to shove the creamy filling in at each end with a small teaspoon! Even washing a piping bag need be no problem at all, if you rinse out the piping bag then include it in your next load for a fairly hot wash in your washing-machine.

Whip the cream until quite stiff and carefully stir in the honey and lemon rind and juice. Just fill your piping bag with the cream and squeeze a little filling in each end of each brandy snap. Pile up in a serving dish and serve.

*F*RESH PEACHES OR NECTARINES WITH RASPBERRY SAUCE

S E R V E S

—— 6 ——

This is a most perfect summer pudding, making the most of the fruits which are in season. It is also ideal as a pudding for those who can't eat any dairy produce. It makes a light finale to a summer meal. The sauce can be made several days in advance, if it is more convenient for you, provided that it is kept covered in the fridge.

INGREDIENTS

6 peaches or *nectarines*
450 g (1 lb) fresh
* raspberries*
50 g (2 oz) icing sugar

Have a pan of boiling water on the heat and stick a fork into each peach or nectarine and dip each into the boiling water for just a few seconds. (I count to 10.) The skin should slip off easily. Cut each in half, and flick out the stones. Lay them cut side down on a pretty serving plate or dish. Put the raspberries into a liquidizer with the icing sugar and whiz till smooth. Sieve this purée over the peach or nectarine halves. You really have to sieve because I have never yet come across a sufficiently sharp-bladed liquidizer which is capable of breaking down the little woody pips in raspberries. Serve.

LEMON AND GINGER SYLLABUB

SERVES

— 6 —

600 ml (1 pint) double cream
Juice of 1 lemon
150 ml (5 fl oz) ginger wine
6 pieces of preserved ginger, drained
Grated rind of 2 lemons

This is a variation on the traditional lemon syllabub, using ginger wine instead of white wine or sherry as the alcohol content. The tastes of lemon and ginger go together so beautifully and I like to serve this with crisp ginger biscuits.

Whip the cream with the lemon juice and the ginger wine. Chop the preserved ginger, and stir this and the lemon rind into the cream. Divide between 6 serving glasses or pots. Keep them in the fridge, covered, till you are ready to serve them.

COFFEE JELLY WITH AMARETTI CREAM

SERVES
—— 6–8 ——

This is a pudding, or dessert, in two parts – the strong coffee jelly accompanied by the whipped cream containing crushed macaroons, or Amaretti, those delicious little almond biscuits which are now easily obtainable from delicatessens and good supermarkets. You can also make each part of the pudding on separate occasions to suit your time. This can be served in two ways, either in two separate dishes, or in one dish in two layers – the coffee jelly covered with the Amaretti cream, but if you do the latter remember to ask your guests to dig deeply!

INGREDIENTS

1½ sachets gelatine
3 tablespoons cold water
900 ml (1½ pints) strong
  black coffee, sweetened
  to taste

FOR THE CREAM:
6 Amaretti biscuits, crushed
  into small chunks
300 ml (10 fl oz) double
  cream, lightly whipped

Sprinkle the gelatine over the water and heat gently in a small pan till the gelatine dissolves. Mix the dissolved gelatine into the coffee and pour this into a serving bowl. Leave to cool and set.

Fold the crushed Amaretti biscuits into the whipped cream, and spread over the surface of the set jelly. Serve.

CHOCOLATE OATMEAL BISCUIT CREAM

SERVES
— 6–8 —

1 packet of oatmeal biscuits
450 ml (15 fl oz) double
cream, whipped
75 g (3 oz) dark chocolate,
grated

This pudding takes about 3 minutes to assemble using your favourite bought oatmeal biscuits.

Spread each biscuit with a little cream, sandwich them together in a long roll on a serving dish. Spread the rest of the whipped cream over the roll and sprinkle with grated chocolate. Serve.

CHOCOLATE MERINGUE CAKE

SERVES
—— 6–8 ——

This meringue is foolproof. It takes 5–7 minutes to make, 2 hours to cook (in a cool oven) and can be made a day in advance – filled with whipped cream a couple of hours before it is to be eaten – or it can be filled and then frozen for a later date. It is delicious.

Pre-heat the oven to gas mark ¼, 225°F (110°C).

Put the whites and sieved icing sugar into a bowl over a saucepan of simmering water. Whisk – I use a hand-held electric whisk for this – till the meringue forms stiff peaks. Take off the heat, and fold in the sieved cocoa using a large metal spoon.

Lay a piece of baking parchment onto a baking tray and mark out two circles on it, by pencilling around a plate about 18 cm (7 in) in diameter. Divide the meringue between the circles, smoothing it evenly. Bake for 2 hours. Cool on a wire rack.

To fill, whip the cream and sandwich together the meringue halves using two-thirds of it. Spread the rest of the cream on top or, if you prefer, pipe rosettes around the edges. Sprinkle the grated dark chocolate over the cream and serve.

INGREDIENTS

3 egg whites
175 g (6 oz) icing sugar, sieved
1 tablespoon cocoa powder, sieved (not drinking chocolate)

FOR THE FILLING:
450 ml (15 fl oz) double cream
50 g (2 oz) grated dark chocolate

PEARS IN
CHOCOLATE MOUSSE

SERVES
— 6 —

175 g (6 oz) good dark chocolate, broken into bits
½ teaspoon vanilla essence or 2 teaspoons instant coffee granules
50 g (2 oz) butter, preferably unsalted
50 g (2 oz) caster sugar
4 eggs, separated
6 ripe juicy pears

Pears go with two things extremely well – ginger and chocolate. In this recipe sliced pears are in the bottom of a dish of rich chocolate mousse. The chocolate mousse will only be as good as the chocolate with which you make it – here speaks a complete and self-confessed chocolate addict! The pudding can be made a day ahead.

Put the chocolate into a heatproof bowl with the vanilla or coffee granules, the butter and sugar. Over a pan of barely simmering water melt the chocolate and butter, mixing together well with a wire whisk. Take the bowl off the heat, and whisk in the egg yolks, one by one. In a separate bowl and with a clean whisk beat the whites till they are stiff, then fold them quickly and thoroughly through the warm chocolate mixture.

Meanwhile, peel, core and slice the pears. Put them in a glass or china dish, and pour the chocolate mousse over. Cover and leave in a fridge till you are ready to serve it.

APRICOT FOOL WITH MARRONS GLACÉS

S E R V E S

— 6 —

You can leave the marrons glacés out of this recipe if you prefer. I include them only as a decoration but they are such a complementary taste to the apricots that I love them. You can make this fool a day in advance, and you can cook the dried apricots and purée them 3–4 days in advance, so it couldn't be simpler to make, or more convenient. I like to serve it in individual glasses.

INGREDIENTS

450 g (1 lb) dried apricots
Pared rind of 1 lemon
100 g (4 oz) caster sugar
Juice of 1 orange
300 ml (10 fl oz) double
  cream, whipped
6 marrons glacés

Put the apricots into a saucepan with water to cover them, and with the lemon rind and sugar. Cover and cook till the apricots are soft, then cool.

Strain the cooking liquid off. Liquidize (lemon rind too) and then stir the orange juice into the apricot purée. Fold in the whipped cream. Divide between 6 serving dishes or glasses, halve each marron and put the two halves on the middle of each serving.

ATHOLL BROSE

INGREDIENTS

600 ml (1 pint) double
cream
3 tablespoons honey,
preferably runny
3 tablespoons whisky
50 g (2 oz) pinhead
oatmeal, toasted

This is a creamy pud based on a Scottish original. It contains cream whipped with whisky and honey. The other main ingredient is oatmeal. Now, when I make this I like to use pinhead oatmeal, to which I am deeply attached for all types of recipes both savoury and sweet. But I realize that pinhead oatmeal may need searching for in southern parts of the country, so substitute rolled oats, or porridge oats instead if you can't lay your hands on a supply of delicious almost nutty-tasting pinhead. The other alternatives are medium and fine oatmeal, but both tend to make the cream altogether too stodgy. I like to shake my pinhead or rolled oats in a dry pan over heat for several minutes before cooling them and folding them into the cream – it improves the flavour.

Whip the cream, adding the honey and whisky. Fold in most of the cooled toasted oatmeal – keep a small amount back to sprinkle a little on top of each serving. Divide the cream between 6 serving glasses and sprinkle each with a little toasted oatmeal. Keep in the fridge until ready to serve.

COFFEE JELLY WITH AMARETTI CREAM (page 97)

QUICK SHERRY TRIFLE

S E R V E S

—— 6–8 ——

Trifle varies practically more than any other dish, but for my taste the simpler the better. What I personally loathe is the sort of trifle where the sponge base is set with fruit jelly which has a sort of syllabub top. For me, trifle should have sponge – cake or fingers – spread with good raspberry or strawberry jam, lots of medium sherry, eggy vanilla custard and whipped cream. For this speedy version, I use custard powder, but I make it up using half the amount specified on the tin to the same amount of liquid, and instead of milk I use single cream. I also add a few drops of vanilla essence. The bananas are an optional extra which I recommend!

———

Arrange the sponge fingers over the base of a serving dish or bowl. Spread the jam over the sponge. Sprinkle the sherry over. If you are including bananas add them at this point. Add the vanilla essence to the custard and pour it over the sponge base. It doesn't matter if it is still hot, providing that, if you are using a glass bowl you add it carefully so as not to break the glass. Leave to cool, then spread the whipped cream over the surface. If you are decorating, scatter the toasted flaked almonds around the edges.

INGREDIENTS

1 packet sponge fingers
1 × 450 g (1 lb) pot raspberry or strawberry jam
150 ml (5 fl oz) medium sherry
3–4 bananas, peeled and sliced (optional)
600 ml (1 pint) custard, (see recipe introduction)
½ teaspoon vanilla essence
300 ml (10 fl oz) double cream, lightly whipped
Toasted flaked almonds to decorate (optional)

FRESH PEACHES OR NECTARINES
WITH RASPBERRY SAUCE (page 95)

RASPBERRY CREAM BRULÉE

SERVES

—— 6–8 ——

750 g (1½ lb) fresh raspberries
450 ml (15 fl oz) double cream, whipped
Caster or granulated sugar

This is one of the simplest puds. I think it is actually easier than serving fresh raspberries with separate cream and sugar because in this dish you have all three items in one. The only thing to remember is to leave it in the fridge till the last moment before grilling the sugar, to prevent the cream rising up over the sugar as it caramelizes.

Put the raspberries into a heatproof dish. Spread the whipped cream over the raspberries and cover the dish with clingfilm, and put it into the fridge for several hours. If you are short of time, don't cover the dish and put it into the freezer for 20–30 minutes. An hour or so before serving it, heat the grill till it is red-hot. Take the dish out of the fridge or freezer and cover the surface with a layer of caster or granulated sugar right up to the edges and to a depth of about 3 mm (⅛ in). Put the dish under the grill and melt the sugar. Keep a close eye on it so that the sugar doesn't burn, and so that the cream doesn't bubble up through the sugar. Serve immediately.

Chocolate Brandy Syllabub

SERVES

—— 6 ——

If you prefer, you can alter the alcohol in this recipe to a liqueur of your choice – a coffee-based one is good, or an orangey one, such as Cointreau. If you prefer to cook without alcohol, substitute strong black coffee, cooled, with sugar stirred into the coffee. I like the flecks of grated chocolate through the cream, but the cream must not be whipped too stiffly as otherwise the grated chocolate will make it almost too solid to dish into the glasses. I don't think it needs any embellishment in the way of decoration, but I do like to serve it with crisp biscuits, either vanilla-, almond- or coffee-flavoured.

INGREDIENTS

600 ml (1 pint) double cream
3 tablespoons brandy
100 g (4 oz) good dark chocolate, grated

Whip the cream, not too stiffly, adding the brandy as you whip. Fold in the grated chocolate, and dish into 6 individual glasses or pots. Coffee cups make an ideal container for this. Keep in the fridge until ready to serve.

CARAMEL BANANA CREAM

SERVES

—— 6–8 ——

INGREDIENTS

175 g (6 oz) granulated
   sugar
900 ml (1½ pints) custard,
   made up according to the
   instructions on the tin
½ teaspoon vanilla essence
300 ml (10 fl oz) double
   cream, lightly whipped
8 bananas

For those of you who are like me and my two sisters in your tastes, this is a heavenly combination – it is a glorified banana custard. It is also a more elegant version of the nursery pudding so many of us love(d). The caramel should be made and then crushed when cold while the custard is cooling. If you want to get ahead you can make the custard, then dampen a bit of greaseproof paper with cold water and press it over the surface of the custard so that it cools without forming a skin. (If you really want to cheat, you can buy cartons of good custard from the supermarket.)

Put the sugar into a wide and heavy-based saucepan and melt over the heat, shaking but not stirring, until the sugar is a molten golden brown. Butter a baking tray and pour the caramel into it. Cool. Then cover with a sheet of greaseproof paper (to prevent the bits flying everywhere) and bash the cold caramel with a rolling pin till it is fairly well crushed.

   Mix together the cooled custard, the vanilla, and the whipped cream. Peel and then slice the bananas into it. Put this combination into a serving bowl, and scatter the crushed caramel over the surface. Keep in the fridge until you are ready to serve. The longer it sits the more the caramel will seep into the creamy mixture – delicious.

PEARS WITH BUTTERSCOTCH SAUCE

S E R V E S

— 6 —

This is a particular favourite with all our family, but with my husband Godfrey especially. You can serve it warm or cold, but if you serve it warm, it is even better if accompanied by vanilla ice-cream. Choose ripe pears because they need to be soft enough without cooking for this recipe.

In a saucepan over gentle to moderate heat dissolve the sugar in the water. Stir in the butter and lemon peel and simmer for 5 minutes. Then fish out the lemon peel. Mix the arrowroot with 2 teaspoons cold water and stir a little of the hot sugar and water into it. Stir this into the contents of the pan, and add the vanilla essence. Stir till the sauce boils. Meanwhile, peel the pears, core and slice them, and lay them in a serving dish. Pour the sauce over the sliced pears and serve warm or cold.

INGREDIENTS

FOR THE SAUCE:
175 g (6 oz) soft dark brown sugar or molasses sugar
150 ml (5 fl oz) water
50 g (2 oz) butter
A long pared piece of lemon rind
1 teaspoon arrowroot
½ teaspoon vanilla essence

6 large, ripe pears

THE BEST UNCOOKED CHOCOLATE FUDGE CAKE

SERVES
—— 6–8 ——

225 g (8 oz) good dark chocolate, broken into bits

225 g (8 oz) unsalted butter, cut into bits

3 tablespoons brandy or black coffee

50 g (2 oz) caster sugar

A few drops of vanilla essence

225 g (8 oz) digestive biscuits, crushed to crumbs

75 g (3 oz) sultanas or 3–4 pieces stem ginger, chopped

75 g (3 oz) walnuts or pecans, chopped

A few whole walnuts or pecans to decorate (optional)

The immodest but truthful name of this pudding separates it from the numerous other recipes for this type of uncooked 'cake'. As ever, the better the dark chocolate you use, the better will be the end result. But this recipe is my father's favourite and as he is the greatest chocolate lover I know (I come a close second) I reckon that that speaks for itself! The 'cake' can be made up to 4 days in advance and kept in the fridge till needed.

Line a loaf tin along the base and up the narrow sides with baking parchment. Put the chocolate, butter, brandy or coffee, caster sugar and vanilla essence into a saucepan over a gentle heat till the butter and chocolate have melted and all is a runny, smooth mixture. Mix in the crushed digestives, the sultanas or ginger, and the chopped nuts, stirring well. Put this into the lined loaf tin and leave to cool. Turn out to serve, peeling off the strip of paper, and decorate, if you like, with a row of whole pecans or walnuts down the centre. Slice to serve.

DIGESTIVE AND CINNAMON PIE WITH BLACKBERRY FILLING

SERVES
—— 6–8 ——

The cinnamon in this pie base brings out the taste of the blackberries in the smooth and creamy filling. I suppose this could technically be called a cheesecake, because it contains cream cheese, but on tasting it you would never know it. The pie can be made a day in advance.

Pre-heat the oven to gas mark 4, 350°F (180°C).

Mix all the pie base ingredients together and press round the sides and base of a flan dish measuring about 23 cm (9 in) in diameter. Bake for 10 minutes. Take out of the oven and cool.

Meanwhile, put the blackberries and sugar in a pan and heat till the juices run – about 2–3 minutes. Sprinkle the gelatine over the lemon juice and, off the heat, stir into the blackberries till the gelatine dissolves in the heat of the fruit. Cool. Whiz in a food processor, adding the cream cheese. In a bowl whisk the egg whites till stiff, then, still whisking, add the sugar a spoonful at a time. Fold together the blackberry mixture with the whisked whites. Pour and scrape into the cooled digestive pie crust. Leave in a cool place – larder or fridge – till needed.

INGREDIENTS

FOR THE PIE BASE:
1 packet of digestive biscuits, crushed to crumbs
75 g (3 oz) butter, melted
50 g (2 oz) demerara sugar
2 teaspoons ground cinnamon

FOR THE FILLING:
450 g (1 lb) blackberries
100 g (4 oz) granulated sugar
1 sachet gelatine
3 tablespoons lemon juice
225 g (8 oz) half-fat cream cheese
2 egg whites
50 g (2 oz) caster sugar

LYCHEES IN CRÈME DE MENTHE

SERVES

— 3 —

INGREDIENTS

1 tin lychees
150 ml (5 fl oz) Crème de
*   Menthe*

This is one of those puddings which takes as long to make as it takes you to open a tin. It is a refreshing and light end to a spur-of-the-moment lunch or dinner. I do have to admit that the idea isn't originally mine. Many years ago my husband Godfrey and I had this pud in a restaurant, but I can't remember now just where!

Empty the contents of the tin, juice and all, into a glass serving bowl. Stir in the Crème de Menthe.

The longer this sits, the more the actual fruit take on the hue and flavour of the Crème de Menthe. If you have time, chill the bowl and its contents in the fridge before serving, or stir in a couple of ice cubes to quick-chill if it is made at the last minute.

CHOCOLATE BREAD CREAM

SERVES
— 6 —

This is a rather off-putting name for one of the most delicious recipes in this book. When I first tasted this pudding, at my sister Camilla's, I was quite unable to analyse the ingredients. She was given the recipe by Susie Priestley who kindly said she didn't mind me using it in this book. In fact, I have made one major alteration to the original, which for my intensely chocolatey passion makes the dish even better. It takes about 3 minutes to make, but it has to be made a day in advance – or at the latest, in the morning for dinner that evening, and kept, covered, in the fridge.

Lightly whip the cream together with the vanilla essence. Mix together the breadcrumbs, demerara sugar, coffee granules and cocoa powder well. In a serving dish layer up the dry mixture and the whipped cream ending with a layer of cream. Grate the chocolate, using a potato peeler, all over the surface. Cover the dish with clingfilm, and put it in the fridge for several hours or overnight.

INGREDIENTS

300 ml (10 fl oz) double cream
1 teaspoon vanilla essence
75 g (3 oz) brown bread, made into fine crumbs
75 g (3 oz) demerara sugar
1 tablespoon instant coffee granules
2 tablespoons cocoa powder (not *drinking chocolate*)
Dark chocolate to decorate

MELITA'S LEMON PUDDING

SERVES

— 6 —

INGREDIENTS

6 trifle sponges or 12
  sponge fingers
300 ml (10 fl oz) double
  cream
Juice of 1 lemon
Juice of 1 orange
Grated rind of 2 lemons
Grated rind of 1 orange
2 tablespoons demerara
  sugar

Melita is a friend of mine. She is a professional concert pianist and so has little time for cooking. She gave me this recipe which I have very slightly adapted. It is extremely quick to make but needs a few hours in a fridge.

Put the sponges into the bottom of a wide shallow dish. Whip the cream, adding the lemon and orange juices slowly as you whip. Fold in the grated rinds. Spread the cream over the sponges. Sprinkle the demerara sugar evenly over the surface. Leave in the fridge overnight, or even longer, before serving.

ORANGE, RHUBARB AND GINGER CREAM

S E R V E S
—— 6–8 ——

This is a set fruity purée with cream added. The three tastes of orange, rhubarb and ginger all complement each other so well. You can whip the cream while the cooked fruit is cooling. The dish can be made up to three days in advance, but remember to take it out of the fridge and leave at room temperature for an hour before serving. It's good served with crisp ginger biscuits.

Put the rhubarb into a pan. Chop the skinned oranges into chunks and add them to the rhubarb, along with the ginger and the sugar. Cover and cook over a moderate heat till the sugar dissolves in the juice that will seep from the pieces of rhubarb. (There is no need to add any water to the pan.)

When the rhubarb is quite soft take the pan off the heat and stir in the gelatine, which will have 'sponged up' in the water. Stir till the gelatine dissolves in the heat of the rhubarb. Liquidize the rhubarb mixture, and pour the resulting purée into a serving bowl to cool completely before adding the whipped cream. Carefully wipe the sides of the bowl with a piece of kitchen paper, cover and put it in the fridge till required. If you like, you can slice some stem ginger into slivers and scatter them around the edges of the rhubarb cream, as a decoration.

INGREDIENTS

750 g (1½ lb) rhubarb (trimmed weight), chopped into chunks
2 oranges, peeled and skinned
2 teaspoons ground ginger
175 g (6 oz) soft brown sugar
1 sachet gelatine, sprinkled over 3 tablespoons water
300 ml (10 fl oz) cream, lightly whipped
Stem ginger, sliced, to decorate (optional)

GINGER COFFEE CREAM

S E R V E S

— 6 —

2 teaspoons sugar
2 tablespoons strong black
   coffee
450 ml (15 fl oz) double
   cream
1 packet of gingernuts
50–75 g (2–3 oz) dark
   chocolate, grated coarsely

This is one of those puds which can be put together in two or three minutes at breakfast time ready for dinner that evening. It does benefit from sitting for several hours, because the coffee-flavoured cream softens the biscuits, and the grated chocolate 'settles' into the cream. The overall effect is quite sumptuous!

Add the sugar to the coffee and allow to cool. Whip the cream adding the sweetened black coffee. Spread each biscuit with some of the coffee cream, and stick them together placing them on a serving dish. Cover with the remaining whipped cream. Grate the chocolate over all to cover the whole pudding. Keep in the fridge for a few hours before serving.

BLACKCURRANT WHIP

S E R V E S

—— 4–6 ——

This is an elegant pudding and is particularly good for serving to guests who are on a dairy-free diet. It has a mousse-like consistency but contains no cream. The volume comes from a meringue-like combination of egg whites and sugar.

There is no need to top and tail the blackcurrants as they are liquidised and sieved in the recipe.

INGREDIENTS

450 g (1 lb) blackcurrants
2 teaspoons gelatine
2 tablespoons lemon juice
3 large egg whites
175 g (6 oz) caster sugar

Cook the blackcurrants by heating them gently in a pan till the juices run – there is no need to add water. The currants are ready when they are quite juicy and soft when pressed against the sides of the pan with the back of a wooden spoon. Sprinkle the gelatine over the lemon juice, then add to the blackcurrants. Stir for a couple of seconds (the gelatine will dissolve in the heat of the blackcurrants). Liquidise, then sieve the purée. Cool.

Whisk the egg whites until stiff then, still whisking, gradually add the sugar, a spoonful at a time. Whisk until you have a stiff meringue. Using a large metal spoon, fold together the meringue mixture and the cooled black-currant purée. Serve in a bowl, or in individual glasses.

S AUCES

A sauce is probably the quickest way of concocting a pudding in a rush –
providing that you have something to serve the sauce with! The most usual
item to sauce would be a tub of good vanilla ice-cream, tucked away in your
freezer. The ingredients for these various sauces can all be found on your
store-cupboard shelves, and I don't think any one of these recipes takes more
than 5 minutes to make (in most cases it's nearer 3). There is only one item
necessary for one of the sauces (the one most popular with all children I know)
that I find impossible to keep in stock – Mars bars. I have to buy them and turn
them into sauce within minutes of getting them into the house, otherwise they
are eaten – by me!

CONTENTS

FUDGE SAUCE *121*

FRUIT SAUCE *122*

CHERRY JAM SAUCE *123*

PECAN OR WALNUT CARAMEL SAUCE *124*

MARS BAR SAUCE *125*

RICH CHOCOLATE SAUCE *126*

FUDGE SAUCE

This recipe has appeared in two of my previous cookbooks, but I make no apology for including it in this one too. It belongs here for two reasons. One is that it is far and away the best recipe for fudge sauce I've come across (it was made by my grandmother's cook, but I don't think she put vanilla into the sauce – I do) and the second reason is that it's quick. Any left over keeps beautifully in the fridge, and also, for left-over use, see the recipe in the Frozen Puddings chapter (see p. 63) – there is fudge ice-cream there!

Put all the ingredients into a saucepan over a gentle to moderate heat and stir till the butter melts and the sugar dissolves. Then boil the sauce for 4–5 minutes. As it boils the sauce thickens. Serve warm.

INGREDIENTS

100 g (4 oz) butter, preferably unsalted
100 g (4 oz) soft brown sugar, light or dark
150 ml (5 fl oz) double cream
About ½ teaspoon vanilla essence

FRUIT SAUCE

SERVES

—— 6 ——

INGREDIENTS

FOR SOFT FRUIT SAUCE:
450 g (1 lb) strawberries
  (hulled), raspberries,
  blackberries
75 g (3 oz) icing sugar
juice 1 orange

**FOR RHUBARB FRUIT
  SAUCE:**
450 g (1 lb) chopped
  rhubarb
75 g (3 oz) soft brown
  sugar
150 ml (5 fl oz) water
rind 1 orange
½ teaspoon ground ginger

**FOR THE GOOSEBERRY
  SAUCE:**
450 g (1 lb) topped and
  tailed gooseberries
75 g (3 oz) caster sugar

The potential of a fruit sauce should never be over-looked. The range is wide, and they are invaluable especially for those who have to keep an eye on their calorie or cholesterol intake. For example, instead of serving whipped cream or ice-cream with an apple pie try a bramble purée – a sauce made simply by liquidizing blackberries (raw or cooked) with icing sugar and a dash of lemon juice, then sieving the purée to get rid of the tiny woody seeds. You can also make a raspberry or straw-berry sauce in the same way. Rhubarb sauce can be made by liquidizing and sieving cooked rhubarb with or with-out ground ginger. It is delicious served with meringues. Gooseberries, cooked, liquidized, sieved and then sweet-ened to taste make an equally good sauce to go with meringues too.

For the soft fruit sauce, liquidize the fruit, sugar and orange juice until a purèe is formed, then sieve to remove the seeds.

For the rhubarb sauce, place the rhubarb, sugar and water in a saucepan and simmer gently until the rhubarb has softened.

Add the grated rind of the orange and the ginger and leave to cool. When cool liquidize.

For the gooseberry sauce, place the fruit in a saucepan and add 4 tablespoons of water. Simmer gently on a low heat until the gooseberries are very soft.

Allow to cool before liquidizing and then sieve to remove the pips. Add the sugar and serve.

CHERRY JAM SAUCE

S E R V E S

—— 6 ——

This is a most useful sauce, and quite delicious, as ever, with vanilla ice-cream. I use Tiptree cherry jam, which I think is one of the best you can get.

If any of this sauce is left over it can be poured back into the pot and kept in the fridge for another time. If you inadvertently spread some on your toast at breakfast, it makes a very special start to the day!

INGREDIENTS

1 × 450 g (1 lb) pot
cherry jam
150 ml (5 fl oz) brandy

Put the two ingredients into a saucepan over a gentle heat and stir occasionally as the jam melts into the brandy.

PECAN OR WALNUT CARAMEL SAUCE

SERVES
— 6 —

INGREDIENTS

100 g (4 oz) butter
100 g (4 oz) granulated
  sugar
1 tablespoon golden syrup
3 tablespoons milk
A few drops of vanilla
  essence

This takes about 10 minutes to make and, although good with vanilla ice-cream, is especially delicious with coffee ice-cream.

Put all the ingredients into a saucepan and stir them over a gentle heat till the butter has melted and the sugar dissolved. Boil the sauce for 5 minutes, stirring. This sauce keeps warm indefinitely.

MARS BAR SAUCE

SERVES

— 6 —

This is just about our children's most favourite sauce to eat with ice-cream. I have to admit that it always goes down extremely well with those further up in years too. The only drawback to this sauce is that you do need an awful lot of Mars bars to make enough sauce to satisfy the demand. For this recipe you need the ordinary, not jumbo, size Mars bars. To make the sauce even better you can use single cream instead of the milk.

INGREDIENTS

6 Mars bars
150 ml (5 fl oz) milk

Measure the milk into a heavy-based saucepan. Cut the Mars bars into bits and put them into the pan with the milk or cream. Over a gentle to moderate heat – don't be tempted to turn the heat up too high – melt the Mars bars in the milk, stirring occasionally. This sauce will keep warm without spoiling for an hour or even two. There is no point my even mentioning what to do with any left-over sauce, because there just never is any left over!

Rich chocolate sauce

SERVES

— 6 —

75 g (3 oz) good dark chocolate
300 ml (10 fl oz) single cream
A few drops of vanilla essence

This is rich but quick. You really have to use very good dark chocolate. The vanilla is optional. If you like, you can add a teaspoonful of instant coffee granules to the cream and chocolate, or a grating of orange rind. If you have any left-over sauce and want to use it another day reheat it gently. If you have stored the left-over sauce in a jar, a good way to reheat the sauce is to put the jar with its lid off in a saucepan of very hot water.

Break the chocolate into tiny bits or grate it – hold the chocolate in foil as you grate it to help prevent the chocolate melting fast against the heat of your hand. Put the cream into a saucepan and add the chocolate and the vanilla essence. Over a gentle to moderate heat – but *not* a high heat as the chocolate will scorch – stir until the cream heats and the chocolate melts. This sauce will thicken as it cools.

INDEX

Italic page numbers refer to colour photographs

A

Alcohol 11, 13
Almonds, strawberry and almond
  cream 88
Amaretti cream, coffee jelly with
  97, *103*
Apples
  apple and cinnamon tart 54, *70*
  apples in butterscotch 50
  autumn pudding 25, *34*
  baked apples stuffed with dates
    56
  blackberry, apple and lemon
    jelly 27
  spiced apple and honey mousse
    37
Apricots
  apricot fool with marrons glacés
    101
  baked dried apricots with orange
    and ginger 45, *68*
Atholl brose 102
Autumn pudding 25, *34*

B

Bananas
  baked in rum, lime and
    cinnamon butter 59
  banana–filled pancakes with
    fudge sauce 92
  caramel banana cream 108
  honey, banana and yoghurt
    ice-cream 64
  strawberry and banana fool 23
Blackberries
  autumn pudding 25, *34*
  blackberry, apple and lemon
    jelly 27
  digestive and cinnamon pie with
    blackberry filling 111
  pear and bramble oatmeal fudge
    crumble 58
Blackcurrants
  blackcurrant whip 117

lemon and blackcurrant water ice
  75
Brambles *see* Blackberries
Brandy 11
  chocolate brandy syllabub 107
Brandy snaps, lemon cream-filled
  94
Bread puddings
  autumn pudding 25, *34*
  chocolate bread cream 113
  rich and quick bread and butter
    pudding 42
Brownies mocha 32
Butterscotch
  apples in 50
  pears with 109

C

Cakes
  baked spiced pineapple 53
  the best uncooked chocolate
    fudge cake 110
  chocolate meringue cake 99
  ice-cream cakes 71–3
  meringue cake 73
  pineapple and pecan spiced 48
  toasted coconut slice 51
  Victoria sponge 72
Caramel
  caramel banana cream 108
  caramel oranges 21
  pecan caramel sauce 122
Cherries
  black cherry creamy delight 31
  cherry jam sauce 123
  cherry yoghurt cream with
    crunchy top 86
Chocolate
  baked vanilla sponge with
    chocolate sauce 52, *69*
  the best uncooked chocolate
    fudge cake 110
  chocolate and coffee junket 20
  chocolate brandy syllabub 107
  chocolate bread cream 113

chocolate marshmallow pie 29
chocolate meringue cream 99
chocolate oatmeal biscuit cream
  98
Mars bar sauce 125
mocha brownies 32
pears in chocolate mousse 100
rich chocolate sauce 126
vanilla and mint chip ice-cream
  65
Coconut slice, toasted 51
Coffee
  chocolate and coffee junket 20
  coffee jelly with Amaretti cream
    97, *103*
  ginger coffee cream 116
  Irish coffee liqueur creams 78
  mocha brownies 32
Cornflakes, golden syrup tart 41
Cranberries
  cranberry and orange water ice 81
  cranberry and orange whip 30
Creams
  Atholl brose 102
  black cherry creamy delight 31
  caramel banana cream 108
  cherry yoghurt cream with
    crunchy top 86
  chocolate bread cream 113
  chocolate oatmeal biscuit cream
    98
  coffee jelly with Amaretti cream
    97, *103*
  cream, yoghurt and grape
    pudding 38
  fresh pineapple and ginger cream
    28
  ginger coffee cream 116
Irish coffee liqueur creams 78
  lemon cream-filled brandy snaps
    94
  lemon rice cream 91
  lychee parfait 90
  Melita's lemon pudding 114
  orange, rhubarb and ginger
    cream 115
  strawberry and almond cream 88

see also Ice-Cream; Syllabubs;
Whips
Cream brûlée
  grape and lemon   89
  rasberry   106
Cream cheese, Edwardian cream   87
Crème de menthe, lychees in   112
Crumbles
  pear and bramble oatmeal fudge
                                  58
  rhubarb with orange   43
Custards
  baked nutmeg custard   49, 68
  caramel banana cream   108
  quick sherry trifle   105

D

Damsons, autumn pudding   25, 34
Dates, baked apples stuffed with 56
Digestive and cinnamon pie with
  blackberry filling   111
Dried fruit salad, hot   60

E

Edwardian cream   87
Elderflower cordial, gooseberry
  and elderflower fool   26
Equipment   15

F

Flavourings   13
Fools
  apricot with marrons glacés   101
  gooseberry and elderfower   26
  strawberry and banana   23
Fromage frais, raspberry whip   36
Frozen puddings   61–81
Fruit
  Edwardian cream   87
  fruit sauce   122
  see also individual types of fruit
Fruit salads
  hot dried fruit salad   60
  hot fresh fruit salad   46
  with honey and lemon dressing
                                  35
Fudge
  banana-filled pancakes with
    fudge sauce   92
  the best uncooked chocolate
    fudge cake   110
  fudge and pecan nut ice-cream 63
  fudge sauce   121

G

Ginger
  baked dried apricots with orange
    and ginger   45, 68

fresh pineapple and ginger cream
                                  28
ginger coffee cream   116
lemon and ginger syllabub   96
orange, rhubarb and ginger
  cream   115
pear and ginger pudding   55
Golden syrup tart   41
Gooseberry and elderflower fool 26
Grapes
  cream, yoghurt and grape
    pudding   38
  grape and lemon brûlée   89

H

Honey
  Atholl brose   102
  fruit salad with honey and lemon
    dressing   35
  honey, banana and yoghurt
    ice-cream   64
  hot fresh fruit salad   46
  iced lemon and honey creams   80
  spiced apple and honey mousse
                                  37

I

Ice-cream
  cakes   71–3
  fudge and pecan nut   63
  honey, banana and yoghurt   64
  iced lemon and honey creams   80
  vanilla and mint chip   65
  vanilla ice and meringue flambé
                                  79
  see also Water ices
Ingredients   11–13
Irish coffee liqueur creams   78

J

Jam sauce, cherry   123
Jellies
  blackberry, apple and lemon   27
  coffee jelly with Amaretti
    cream   97, 103
  fresh orange and chopped
    strawberry   93
Junket   19
  chocolate and coffee   20

L

Lemon
  baked lemon rice pudding   44
  blackberry, apple and lemon
    jelly   27
  grape and lemon brûlée   89

iced lemon and honey creams   80
lemon and blackcurrant water ice
                                  75
lemon and Cointreau water
  ice-filled orange shells   33, 74
lemon and ginger syllabub   96
lemon cream-filled brandy snaps
                                  94
lemon rice cream   91
Melita's lemon pudding   114
pineapple and lemon water ice   76
Liqueur creams, Irish coffee   78
Lychees
  lychee parfait   90
  lychees in crème de menthe   112

M

Mango and orange water ice   66
Marrons glacés, apricot fool with
                                 101
Mars bar sauce   125
Marshmallow pie, chocolate   29
Melita's lemon pudding   114
Melon and Lapsang Souchong tea
  water ice   77
Meringues   24
  chocolate meringue cake   99
  meringue cake   73
  vanilla ice and meringue flambé
                                  79
Milk puddings
  baked lemon rice pudding   44
  baked nutmeg custard   49, 68
  chocolate and coffee junket   20
  junket   19
  lemon rice cream   91
Mincemeat-stuffed pears   57
Mint, vanilla and mint chip ice-
  cream   65
Mocha brownies   32
Mousses
  pears in chocolate mousse   100
  spiced apple and honey   37

N

Nectarines with raspberry sauce 95,
  104
Nutmeg   11
  baked nutmeg custard   49, 68
Nuts   11

O

Oatmeal
  Atholl brose   102
  cherry yoghurt cream with
    crunchy top   86
  chocolate oatmeal biscuit cream
                                  98

pear and bramble oatmeal fudge
    crumble   58
plum nut crunch   47, 67
Oranges
    baked dried apricots with orange
        and ginger   45, 68
    caramel oranges   21
    cranberry and orange water ice
                                    81
    cranberry and orange whip   30
    fresh orange and chopped
        strawberry jelly   93
    lemon and Cointreau water
        ice-filled orange shells 33, 74
    mango and orange water ice 66
    orange, rhubarb and ginger
        cream   115
    rhubarb with orange fudge
        crumble   43

P

Pancakes, banana-filled with fudge
    sauce   92
Parfait, lychee   90
Peaches with raspberry sauce   95,
    104
Pears
    baked mincemeat-stuffed   57
    with mulled wine sauce   22
    pear and bramble oatmeal fudge
        crumble   58
    pear and ginger pudding   55
    pears in chocolate mousse   100
    pears with butterscotch sauce 109
Pecan nuts
    fudge and pecan nut ice-cream 63
    pecan caramel sauce   124
    pineapple and pecan spiced cake
                                    48
Pineapple
    baked spiced pineapple cake   53
    fresh pineapple and ginger cream
                                    28
    pineapple and lemon water ice 76
    pineapple and pecan spiced cake
                                    48
Plum nut crunch   47, 67

R

Raspberries
    fresh peaches with raspberry
        sauce   95, 104
    raspberry cream brulée   106
    raspberry whip   36
Rhubarb
    orange, rhubarb and ginger
        cream   115
    with orange fudge crumble   43
Rice puddings
    baked lemon rice pudding   44
    lemon rice cream   91

S

Sauces   119–25
    butterscotch   109
    cherry jam   123
    chocolate   52
    fruit   122
    fudge   92, 121
    Mars bar   125
    pecan or walnut caramel   124
    rich chocolate   126
Sherry trifle   105
Spices   11
Strawberries
    fresh orange and chopped
        strawberry jelly   93
    strawberry and almond cream 88
    strawberry and banana fool   23
Syllabubs
    chocolate brandy   107
    lemon and ginger   96

T

Tarts
    apple and cinnamon   54, 70
    golden syrup   41
Tea melon and Lapsang Souchong
    tea water ice   77
Trifle, quick sherry   105

V

Vanilla
    baked vanilla sponge with
        chocolate sauce   52, 69
    vanilla and mint chip ice-cream
                                    65
    vanilla ice and meringue flambé
                                    79
Victoria sponge   72

W

Walnuts
    plum nut crunch   47, 67
    walnut caramel sauce   124
Water ices
    cranberry and orange   81
    lemon and blackcurrant   75
    lemon and Cointreau water
        ice-filled orange shells 33, 74
    mango and orange   66
    melon and Lapsang Souchong
        tea   77
    pineapple and lemon   76
    see also Ice-cream
Whips
    blackcurrant   117
    cranberry and orange   30
    raspberry   36
Wine, pears with mulled wine
    sauce   22

Y

Yoghurt
    black cherry creamy delight   31
    cherry yoghurt cream with
        crunchy top   86
    fresh pineapple and ginger cream
                                    28
    honey, banana and yoghurt
        ice-cream   64

JOANNA FARROW'S QUICK AND EASY FISH COOKERY

Is your idea of a quick and easy fish dish limited to fishfingers or fish and chips? If so, *Joanna Farrow's Quick and Easy Fish Cookery* will change all that. Joanna Farrow explodes the myth that cooking with fish is time-consuming and complicated. Her recipes are imaginative, simple to prepare and show how to get the best out of the exciting variety of fish now widely available.

CLARE CONNERY'S QUICK AND EASY SALADS

Imaginative salad recipes for all occasions, compiled in the popular 'quick and easy' format. Sunny Irish cook Clare Connery creates some delicious new salads, as well as spicing up some old favourites.

BEVERLEY PIPER'S QUICK AND EASY HEALTHY COOKERY

A fun, easy-to-read book designed for those who wish to follow a healthy diet but have limited time to cook. Each tasty recipe is accompanied by information about the nutritional value of the ingredients enabling you to cook really well-balanced meals.

SANDEEP CHATTERJEE'S QUICK AND EASY INDIAN VEGETARIAN COOKERY

Sandeep Chatterjee's Quick and Easy Indian Vegetarian Cookery is the first cookbook from Sandeep Chatterjee, the highly acclaimed chef from London's *Bombay Brasserie*. A wonderful introduction to Indian vegetarian food, with recipes which are quick and easy to make.

SARAH BROWN'S QUICK AND EASY VEGETARIAN COOKERY

Sarah Brown's recipes concentrate on main meals, with wholefood, vegetable and salad ingredients as their basis. There is also a chapter on soups and starters, a collection of recipes for delicious desserts and a selection of imaginative menus.

SHAUN HILL'S QUICK AND EASY VEGETABLE COOKERY

Bored with baked potatoes, uninspired by carrots and leeks? Shaun Hill will put the imagination back into your vegetable rack! *Shaun Hill's Quick and Easy Vegetable Cookery* is a celebration of the common vegetable. A well-respected chef in a variety of culinary fields, it is his ability to bring out the individual characteristics of every ingredient that makes Shaun Hill's recipes a must for any cook.

KEN HOM'S QUICK AND EASY CHINESE COOKERY

Ken Hom's best-selling *Chinese Cookery* has become the classic guide to the art of preparing Chinese food. Now, in his *Quick and Easy Chinese Cookery* he makes the most of traditional Chinese quick-cook techniques and shows you how to make mouth-watering and healthy meals in minutes.